BPMN

The Business Process Modeling Notation

Pocket Handbook

Patrice Briol

BPMN – the Business Process Modeling Notation
Pocket Handbook

The BPMN notation, BPMN logo are registered trademarks of Object Management Group (OMG). Object Management Group™, OMG™ are trademarks of the Object Management Group. All other products or company names mentioned are used for identification purposes only, and may be trademarks of their respective owners.

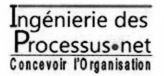

http://www.ingenieriedesprocessus.net

First Edition
ISBN 978-1-4092-0299-8

Contents

Introduction 5

Chapter 1 - Business Process Management 7

Chapter 2 - Business Process Modeling 9

  2.1 Business models..9
  2.2 The Process diagram 13
  2.3 Modeling best practices...14

Chapter 3 - Business Process Modeling Notation...........17

  3.1 Background 17
  3.2 Scope..18
  3.3 Business Process Diagram 19
  3.4 Terminology...23
  3.5 Participants...25
  3.6 The Business Processes types 28
  3.7 Flow Objects 33
    3.7.1 Events...33
      Start Event...35
      End Event...37
      Intermediate Event 39
    3.7.2 Activities 43
      Activity..43
      Task..45
      Loop 47
      Sub-Processes...49
    3.7.3 Gateways...54
      Exclusive Gateway..55
      Inclusive Gateway..58
      Complex Gateway..59
      Parallel Gateway 60
  3.8 Connecting objects...62
    3.8.1 Sequence Flow 63
    3.8.2 Message Flow..67
    3.8.3 Association..69
    3.8.4 The Compensation Association............................69
  3.9 The Artifacts 72
    3.9.1 Data Object..72
    3.9.2 Group 74
    3.9.3 Annotation..74

3.10 Business Process modeling with BPMN 75

Chapter 4 - Workflow Patterns 79

4.1 The Sequence 81
4.2 The Parallel Split 81
4.3 The Synchronization 83
4.4 The Exclusive Choice 84
4.5 The Simple Merge 85
4.6 The Multiple Choice 86
4.7 The Multiple Merge 87
4.8 The Discriminator 88
4.9 The N out M Join 89
4.10 The Synchronizing Merge 90
4.11 The Arbitrary Cycles 91
4.12 The Implicit Termination 92
4.13 The Multiples Instances with a priori Design Time Knowledge 92
4.14 The Multiples Instances with a priori Runtime Knowledge 93
4.15 The Multiples Instances with no a priori Knowledge 94
4.16 The Multiple Instances requiring Synchronization 95
4.17 The Deferred Choice 95
4.18 The Interleaved Routing 96
4.19 The Milestone 97
4.20 The Cancel Activity 98
4.21 The Cancel Case 99

Chapter 5 - Samples 101

5.1 Incident Management Process 102
5.2 Problem Management Process 103
5.3 Change Management Process 104
5.4 Receive Order Process 105

Chapter 6 - Key differences between v1.0 and v1.1 107

6.1 Graphical Element markers 107
6.2 Events Categories 108
6.3 Signal Event type 109
6.4 Link Event type 110
6.5 Rules Event type 110
6.6 Event Details attribute 110

Figures 113

Tables 117

Index 119

Introduction

This pocket handbook is written for individuals involved in the modeling stage of a Business Process Management (BPM) initiative.

Since its inception, the Business Process Modeling Notation (BPMN) has been adopted and integrated by most of the BPM market players (Intalio, IBM, BEA, Savvion, Sun, etc.) in their modeling tools. This guide intends to help the modelers in their daily job of capturing the Business Processes within their organization.

This BPMN pocket handbook is based on the OMG BPMN specification version 1.0. It describes the Business Process Modeling and its standard notation within six chapters:

- Business Process Management
- Business Process Modeling
- Business Process Modeling Notation
- Workflow Patterns
- Samples
- The key differences between BPMN specification version 1.0 and version 1.1

The complete BPMN specification is available at the OMG's Internet address: http://www.omg.org.

Chapter 1

Business Process Management

The Business Process Management aims to consider the current enterprise organization as a set of coordinated and managed activities executed in a determined order to reach common objectives defined at the enterprise's strategy level.

A Business Process is a set of coordinated activities executed by the organizational units of the enterprise. These activities are either manual or automated tasks.

The Business Process Management initiative requires at least three stages:

- The analysis and design of Business Processes in order to reach the strategic objectives.
- The implementation and execution of Business Processes.
- The monitoring of Business Processes and the definition of correctives actions.

As illustrated in the Figure 1.1, these stages complete a Business Process Management life cycle.

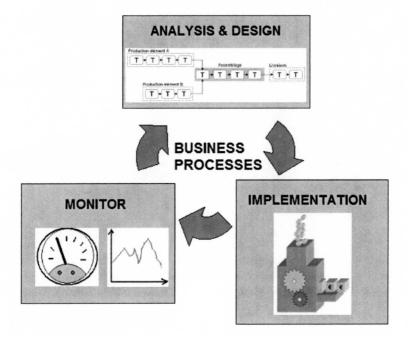

Figure 1.1 – Business Process Management life cycle

The Business Processes analysis and design stage requires an important amount of human interactions and communication. The Business Analyst has to understand and report their perceptions of the reality of the organization's situation to the involved stakeholders. There are several format representations to report Business Process information. The graphical one is the most practical, easiest and fastest way to maintain, understand and communicate the information. The Business Process Modeling aims to produce Business Process models in a business-oriented details level.

Chapter 2

Business Process Modeling

The first stage of the BPM life cycle focuses on gathering the organization's information and its way of running and producing benefits. The amount of collected information may introduce some complexity depending on the number of stakeholders, hierarchical levels, tasks, interactions and messages exchanged. The Business Process modeling will significantly reduce that complexity.

2.1 Business models

A model is an abstraction of reality. It functions, in a dedicated way, to reduce the natural complexity of the reality it represents. A Business Process model identifies the essential elements that drive the business, such as the endogenous and exogenous factors acting upon the organization's way of working, and eventually, on the enterprise's result.

A model may have many representations as worksheet or graphical diagrams. It is important to distinguish the difference between a *model* and a *diagram.* A model captures sufficient information about a studied phenomenon to simulate the reality. A diagram is a graphical representation of the phenomenon to help the understanding and the communication of the reality's perspectives. The Process of *cartography* groups together all Business Process diagrams organized by levels of information.

A Business Process model may illustrate various aspects of the organization:

- Finance
- Resources usage
- Information technology architecture
- Organization
- Production
- Accounting
- Marketing and sales
- Activities localization
- Etc.

According to the customer's needs, the Business Analyst may favor one of these aspects in their drafted models. Then, each stage of the BPM lifecycle will use these models as a reference for all measures and improvement actions. The models may also be used to build some theoretical alternative improvement scenarios evaluated within a simulation mechanism provided by the modeling tool.

The Enterprise's referential is built on the top of these models and may be used to automatically produce the organization's procedures in conformance with a quality standard like the ISO9000.

There are many ways to represent the same information. A dedicated perspective represents one particular view of the organization according to its objectives and usages. The choice of available diagrams depends on some criteria:

- The design methodology and principles.
- The modeling tool.
- The stakeholders and the individuals involved within the organization's Business Processes.
- The enterprise's communication tool.
- The diagram's notation.

There is no absolute rule to model the Business Processes. However, there are several fundamental diagrams and models to illustrate the current situation of the organization:

- The Business Process diagram describes the logical and chronological sequences of its activities.
- The Value Chain diagram depicts a macroscopic view of the value creation within the organization.
- The Organization Chart represents the hierarchical organizational structure.
- The Business Rules sheets define the applied rules and policies within the organization.

The complexity of the enterprise's current Business Processes may naturally incite the creation of a large amount of models and diagrams. Despite the simplification of the reality with modeling usage, the model number may add complexity to the process of searching and finding detailed information. It is important to focus on the Business Processes' information organization when starting a BPM initiative. The enterprise referential may compose some dedicated levels of details as illustrated in Figure 2.1.

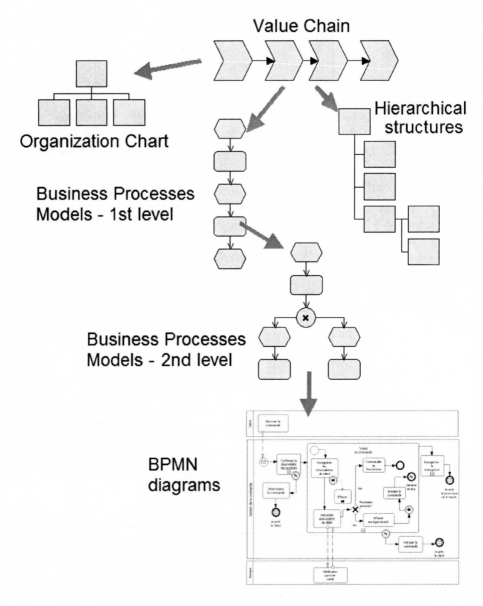

Figure 2.1 – Business Processes information levels

2.2 The Process diagram

The Process diagram visually describes the logical and chronological sequences of activities. Independently from the retained modeling notation, the Process diagram is always composed of several fundamental graphical elements:

- Tasks
- Events
- Information
- Business Rules

The concept of a "token" flowing through the Process' activities helps the design, reading and understanding of the Process diagrams. The idea behind the token is that a fragment of information passing through the activities creates a flow representing the Process execution itself. The token path depends on the scenarios and their data. The same Process may have many possible token flows according to the sequential and concurrent Sequence Flows within the Process as illustrated in Figure 2.2. The token activates the activity when it passes through. When the activity is finished, the token is freed and transmitted to the next activity.

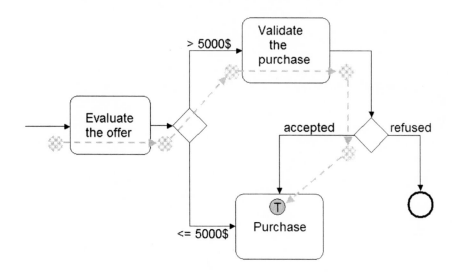

Figure 2.2 – Token flow between activities

The token is created by the first activity each time the Process starts. It contains basic and structured information with global data scope used and updated along the Process execution. These data may also be used to determine the path to follow. A token also has the possibility to fork itself - to go through simultaneous paths - and later synchronize to continue on a single path until the Process ends. The latest activity consumes the tokens and the Process terminates.

The activities produce an outgoing result from incoming raw material or information. They are both considered as *Object*. According to the modeling methodology, an *activity* is equivalent to a *task* or a *work item*.

The Process diagram is a representation of possible flows between some activities.

There are two generic flow types within the Business Process diagram:

- The *Sequence Flow* represents the possible activity execution sequences within the Business Process. A Sequence Flow execution depends on the token values and applied Business Rules.
- The *Object Flow* represents the path used by an Object in the Process execution. That flow is not necessarily the same as the Sequence Flow. Any activity is able to modify the Object properties.

2.3 Modeling best practices

The success of the Business Process modeling depends on several criteria. Before the inception of a modeling initiative, it is necessary to verify some important issues:

- The enterprise top management has to be formally involved in order to ensure the access to the whole organization information and their support of the BPM initiative within the organization.
- It is necessary to have the sufficient modeling means associated with a models maintenance plan containing all updates, even after their implementation.
- The model is business oriented, aiming to serve and improve the business. The Business Analyst intentionally omits the technical details and focuses only on business issues of the Processes.
- The model has to be enough complete including an exhaustive level of information that satisfies the business needs. The model helps the understanding and communication of the Business Process information in order to improve their efficiency.

- It is necessary to acquire all Business Process aspects and not only their compound activities.
- It is necessary to select a good modeling tool supporting the graphical standard notations.
- The model has to be defined with enough accuracy and without ambiguity.
- It is necessary to plan the information gathering with the key people in the targeted organization.
- The completed and validated models have to be easily translatable in real actions.
- The model has to contain several perspectives according to the stakeholders' needs and categories.
- The model has to support a quick Processes implementation to meet the stakeholders' needs.
- The model has to be refined iteratively by following the Business Rules evolution with a frequent matching evaluation between the initial needs and the current controlled situation.

Chapter 3

Business Process Modeling Notation

3.1 Background

In 2004, the Business Process Management Initiative (BPMI.org) developed and published the Business Process Modeling Notation (BPMN) version 1.0. In 2006, the BPMI gave the rights to maintain the BPMN notation to the Object Management Group (OMG), a not-for-profit computer industry standards consortium. The OMG owns many specifications including UML, CORBA, CWM and other industry-specific standards for dozens of vertical markets. In January 2008, the OMG released the BPMN version 1.1.

The BPMN standard notation consolidates the best ideas from other notations including UML activity diagram, IDEF, ebXML BPSSm ADF, Event-Process Chains (EPCs), etc.

The BPMN notation aims to be readily understandable by all business users:

- The Business Analysts who create the initial drafts of the Process diagrams.
- The technical IT developers who implement and integrate the automated Business Process activities.
- The business people who manage and monitor the Business Processes.

The BPMN notation targets other secondary objectives:

- It fills the gap between the Business Process designs and their implementation.
- It ensures that the XML languages designed for the execution of Business Processes (BPEL) are depicted with a business-oriented notation.
- It is a widespread modeling notation.
- It provides an overall information communication mean for all Processes stakeholders.

3.2 Scope

The BPMN specification contains two parts:

- The description of the BPMN visual elements and their usage.
- The mapping between the BPMN visual objects and their translation into a BPM execution language (BPEL4WS). That part is mainly used by BPM market's players to build their technical solution.

The BPMN notation focuses on Business Processes without covering other organizational aspects:

- The organization chart and resources.
- The information data model.
- The enterprise strategy.
- The Business Rules.

The BPMN specification describes two abstraction levels in Business Process modeling:

- A summarized level containing only the core graphical elements set intended to be used by the Business Analyst.
- A detailed level with complementary visual elements and mechanisms mainly used to guarantee a correct Process implementation.

The BPMN specification covers only the description of the notation's elements. It does not provide a definition of specific Business Process design or implementation methodology.

3.3 Business Process Diagram

A Business Process Diagram (BPD) combines the visual objects to depict a Business Process execution in order to fill the stakeholders' needs. These visual objects are mainly organized in flows as illustrated in Figure 3.1.

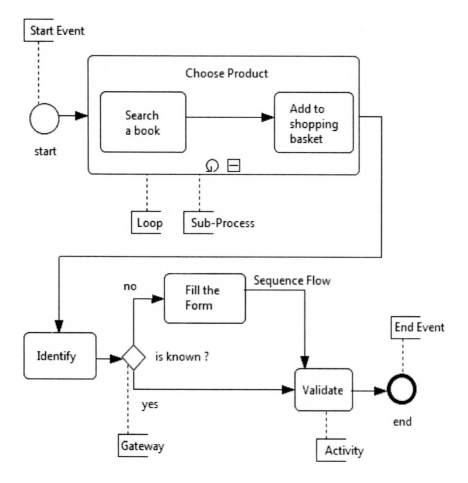

Figure 3.1 – Sample BPD diagram

Each visual object has a distinctive signification or semantic within the BPD diagram. This means that these visual objects are able to influence the Process execution, except for the Annotation Artifact object. Figure 3.2 illustrates the insertion of an Annotation associated with an activity. The Annotation is equivalent to the commentaries described in traditional programming language.

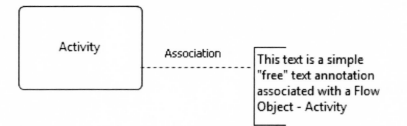

Figure 3.2 – Annotation in a BPD diagram

The BPD core element set (see Table 3.1) addresses the graphical elements within dedicated categories. The modeler may add some variations and information to those core element categories in order to support new requirements without dramatically changing the basic look and feel of the diagram.

Table 3.1 – BPD core element set

Category	Description	Elements
Flow Objects	They are the main graphical elements that define the behavior of a Business Process.	Events Activities Gateways
Connecting Objects	They define the way Flow Objects are connected together.	Sequence Flow Message Flow Association
Swimlines	They depict the Process's Participants and various roles.	Pools Lanes

Category	Description	Elements
Artifacts	They provide additional visual information to help the reading and understanding of the BPD diagrams.	Data Object Group Annotation

Each BPMN element has its own attributes to describe its static and behavioral characteristics. The BPMN specification is flexible enough to allow the addition of new attributes in accordance with some conformance rules:

- The visual appearance of the BPMN graphical elements.
- The semantics of the BPMN elements.
- The exchange of BPMN Diagrams between conformant BPMN modeling tools.

Figure 3.3 illustrates a global overview of the graphical objects available in a BPD Diagram.

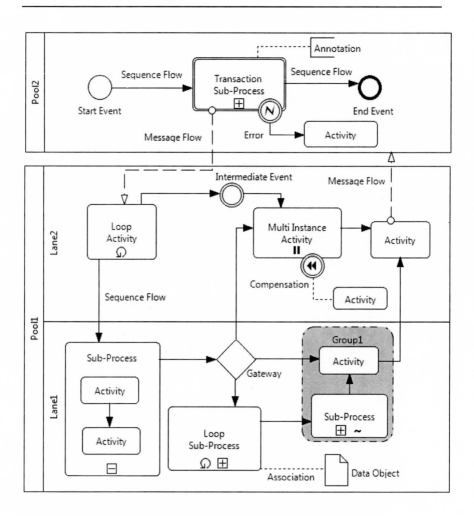

Figure 3.3 – Graphical objects used in a BPD diagram

3.4 Terminology

The BPMN notation's elements description uses a common terminology (see Table 3.2) to avoid confusion with other notations.

Table 3.2 – BPMN terminology

Term	Description
Activity	The Activity is a general term that describes a work item executed within the organization. That work may take many representations like a Process, a Sub-Process or a task.
Alternative Sequence Flow	An Alternative Sequence Flow represents a decision among many alternatives.
Artifact	An Artifact is a simple element of information used to help the reading and understanding of the BPD diagram.
Association	The Association represents the link between the Artifact and other graphical objects (Flow objects and Swimlines).
Business Process	A set of coordinated activities performed within the organizations. For the BPMN specification, a Business Process is displayed within a BPD diagram and contains one or more Processes.
Business Process Diagram (BPD)	The Business Process Diagram (BPD) is defined by the BPMN specification as the diagram containing defined graphical elements.
Concurrent Sequence Flows	Many Sequence Flows simultaneously executed within the Process.
Executable Process	An Executable Process has enough details to be interpreted by individuals and/or automated Business Process Management Systems execution.
Event	An Event is a signal raised during the Business Process execution. The BPMN specification defines a dedicated mechanism representation within the BPD diagram to handle the events signals. The BPMN specification identifies three events types: Start, Intermediate and End Events.

Term	Description
Gateway	A Gateway controls the divergence and convergence of Sequence Flow. It determines branching, forking, merging, and joining of paths from a specified condition. It is represented with a diamond shape.
Message	A Message is structured information used in the Message Flows between the Process' Participants.
Message Flow	A Message Flow depicts the Message exchange link between Participants.
Participant	A Participant is an individual, a business entity or an information system executing the activities of a Process. Each Participant, represented by a Pool, cooperates on the same Process and share several activities.
Process	A Process is any activity performed within an organization. For the BPMN notation, a Process is depicted as a network of Flow Objects. The BPMN specification identifies three types of Processes: Private (internal), Public (abstract) and Collaboration (global).
Process Instance	A Process Instance represents a particular execution of a Business Process having its own attributes values. An instance is created each time the Process is started and it terminates with the end of the Process. A Process may have concurrent Process Instances.
Sequence Flow	The Sequence Flow represents the ordered sequence of activity execution. It is visually illustrated with a solid arrow between Flow Objects.
Sub-Process	A Sub-Process is a Process included within another Process. The BPMN specification defines two Sub-Process representations: the collapsed and the expanded Sub-Process views.
Task	Atomic Activity executed within a Process.

3.5 Participants

A Participant is a business entity, which executes or has responsibilities in the execution of the activities within a Process. For the BPMN notation, a *Pool* visually represents one Participant.

The BPMN specification distinguishes two levels of participation:

- The organizational unit is the internal or external interest group of the organization like the enterprise, the department, the customer, the providers, etc.
- The associated role to the activity execution involved in most of the message exchanges between the organizational units.

A BPD diagram may contain some Pools. A Pool is visually represented with square-cornered rectangle identified by its label as illustrated in Figure 3.4. A Pool will extend the entire length of the BDP, either horizontally or vertically.

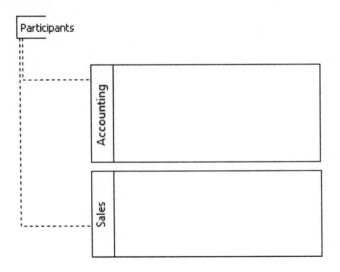

Figure 3.4 – Two Participants in the same BPD diagram

Each Participant carries its own authority and executes any activities within its Pool. On the other hand, the Participant has no authority on the activities located outside the boundaries of its Pool. However, the collaboration between several Participants on the same Business Process is solved with mutual message exchanges (See Figure 3.5). For example, one Participant sends a message to another Participant awaiting the information it needs to be able to continue its own execution. From that point of view, each Participant is able to drive the execution of other Participants' activities.

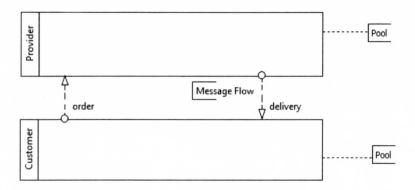

Figure 3.5 – Message flow representation between two Participants

A BPD diagram contains at least one Participant. If it contains only one Participant, it is not mandatory to draw the Pool object as illustrated in the Figure 3.6.

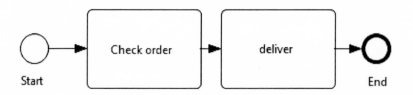

Figure 3.6 – Default BPD diagram Pool object

A "main" Pool is drawn without the boundaries and its activities are considered as "internal" to the organization, while the represented Pool with their boundaries in the same Process describes the "external" activities as illustrated in Figure 3.7.

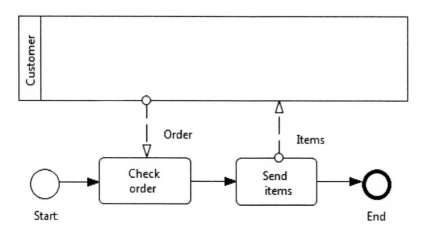

Figure 3.7 – The main BPD Pool

The BPMN notation specifies the representation for the Participant's role as a *Lane* within a Pool. If the Pool contains only one Lane, the latter is not graphically represented. The Lane is only used when the Pool has many Lanes as illustrated in Figure 3.8.

Each role is responsible for the activities executed on its Lane. However, a Sequence Flow may pass through many Lanes to execute the Pool's activities. The Sequence Flow is graphically represented with plains arrows between the activities.

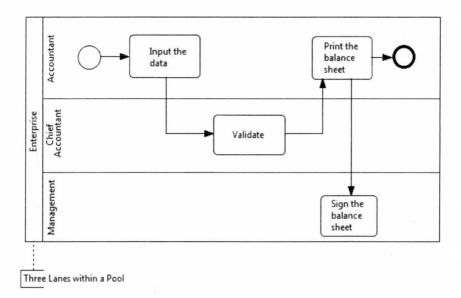

Three Lanes within a Pool

Figure 3.8 – Pool and Lanes within a BPD

3.6 The Business Processes types

The BPMN specification differentiates three categories of Business Processes:

- The Private (internal) Business Process.
- The Public (abstract) Business Process.
- The Collaboration (global) Business Process.

The "Workflow" term is equivalent to the Private (internal) Processes. They are both directly translatable into Process execution language like BPEL4WS. Figure 3.9 depicts an internal Process definition within a default BPD diagram.

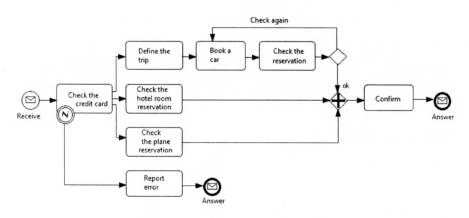

Figure 3.9 – Private (internal) Process

A Private Process may have to be declared within many Participants. Figure 3.10 illustrates the representation of several Private Processes in a BPD diagram.

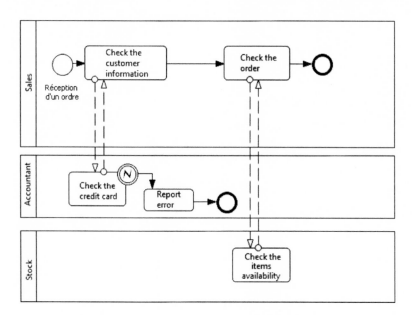

Figure 3.10 – Private Process and their Participants

A Public Process defines the interactions between the activities of several Participants. Only the involved activities of the flow from the different sides are represented. Without specification of the internal activities implementation, the Public Process is non-executable. Figure 3.11 illustrates the Public Process of a Service Desk. Only the *interface* or activities having a relation with the User are defined.

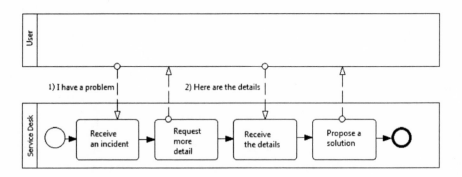

Figure 3.11 – Public (abstract) Process

Any BPD diagram may contain several Public and Private Processes definition as illustrated in Figure 3.12.

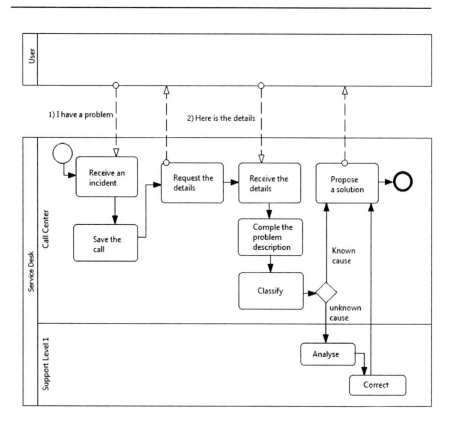

Figure 3.12 – A set of Private and Public Processes

The Collaboration Process focuses on the communication between several Public Processes (See Figure 3.13). It increases the level of abstraction by describing only the message exchanges between several Participants. That level of abstraction does not allow any Process execution.

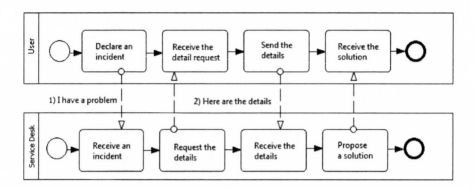

Figure 3.13 – Collaboration (global) Process

The combination of the three main Process categories creates new ones:

- A high-level non-executable Private Process.
- A detailed Private and executable Process.
- The current Business Process situation (AsIs), non-executable.
- The desired Business Process situation (ToBe), non-executable.
- Two or more internal Business Processes interacting together and executable.
- A Private executable Business Processes interacting with Public Processes.
- A Private and detailed Business Process associated with Collaboration Processes.
- Two or more Public Processes.
- Public Processes with Collaboration Processes.
- Etc.

The BPMN notation has been initially designed to answer several Business Process abstraction levels. The split of the main Process into Sub-Processes helps to reduce the BPD complexity.

The BPMN notation also integrates some specifics mechanisms:

- The Transaction support ensuring a complete execution of a defined part of the Sequence Flow.
- The Exception and Error handling of the Process execution.
- The Compensation mechanism used to cancel previously executed activities.

These three mechanisms intend to help the Process implementation with some dedicated execution issues. The IT developer will generally introduce them in the drafted BPD diagrams later in order to implement the Process execution.

3.7 Flow Objects

3.7.1 Events

An Event is something that takes place during the Process Execution and influences the normal Sequence Flow. From a BPMN point of view, the Event is also a representation of a mechanism supporting a dedicated behavior. There are two distinctive Event roles:

- An Event transmitter, which broadcasts the event information.
- An Event listener, which handles the event information to continue the execution of a specialized activity.

A Business Process always starts and ends with an Event. The specification describes three events types:

- The *Start Event* triggers the start of the Process execution with its first activity in the Sequence Flow. The Start Event is always an event's listener. The Start Event initiates the token instantiation within the Sequence Flow.
- The *Intermediate Event* specifies the event triggered during the Business Process execution. The Intermediate Event plays the transmitter role when it is located directly on the Sequence Flow, and the listener role when it is located on the activities' shape boundaries.
- The *End Event* triggers after the termination of the final activity of the Sequence Flow and it is always an event's transmitter. The End Event consumes all incoming tokens arriving from the Sequence Flow.

A circle shape visually represents any Event type. Its outline distinguishes the three Event types as illustrated in Table 3.3.

Table 3.3 – Event types

Event	Outline	Symbol
Start	Single	
Intermediate	Double	
End	Bold	

Figure 3.14 illustrates the three Event types and their common location within a Sequence Flow.

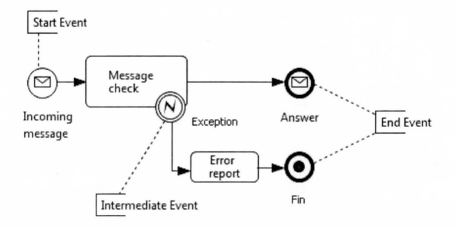

Figure 3.14 – BPMN Events sample

Start Event

A Start Event indicates where a particular Process will start. Within a Sequence, the Start Event object is optional. However, if the Sequence Flow contains at least one End Event, it is necessary to specify a Start Event on the same Process level. As specified before, the Start Event creates a new token each time it triggers.

A Process may contain several Start Events as illustrated in Figure 3.15. The Business Process Management System provides the *Correlation Set* mechanism in order to ensure that all triggered Start Events will apply to the same Process Instance. In Figure 3.15, the activity labeled T5 has the responsibility to transfer the right data to the right Sequence Flow, even if the tokens are simultaneous. The Correlation Set is reserved for the Business Process implementer. There is no graphical object representation of the Correlation Set mechanism.

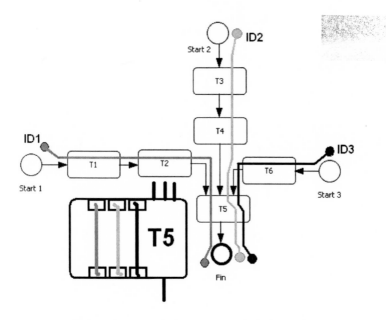

Figure 3.15 – Correlation set mechanism

A Start Event may have a Trigger that indicates how the Process will start. The Trigger is represented with a marker placed in the center of the Event shape as illustrated in Figure 3.16.

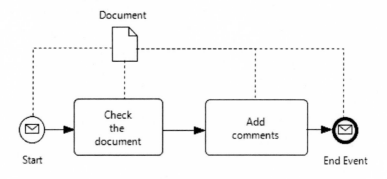

Figure 3.16 – Start Event

Table 3.4 describes the six Start Event types specified in the BPMN notation.

Table 3.4 – The Start Events description and symbol

Type	Symbol	Description
None		The event is triggered without specific description of the trigger. It indicates as well the start of the Sub-Process execution.
Message		The event is triggered when it receives an incoming message from another Participant.
Timer		The event is triggered after a specified amount of time.
Rule		The event is triggered when a defined rule validates the condition.

Type	Symbol	Description
Link		The event is triggered when it receives an incoming token from another Process having triggered the End Link Event. The Link Event is like a "goto" statement in standard programming language.
Multiple		Multiple ways of triggering the Process (Message, Timer, Rule, Link) may start the Process. The Process starts at any one of these event triggers.

End Event

The End Event triggers when the Sequence Flow terminates as illustrated in Figure 3.17. The End Event consumes all tokens when the Process terminates. A dedicated Intermediate Event on Error handling consumes the remaining tokens if an error is thrown during the Sequence Flow execution and the End Event cannot be reached. If the Sequence Flow has no Start or End Event, the latest activity of the Sequence Flow plays the same role as the End Event.

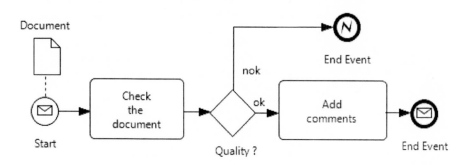

Figure 3.17 – End Event sample

The End Event is an Event transmitter and it broadcasts the information when it is triggered. The BPMN specification defines eight End Event types as described in the Table 3.5.

Table 3.5 – The End Event types

Type	Symbol	Description
None		The None End Event triggers when the Process execution terminates for an unspecified reason. For a Sub-Process, the None End Event indicates the return to the Parent Process.
Message		When triggered, it sends a message to another Participant.
Error		That event triggers a named Error. An Intermediate Error Event must be placed on an activity boundary at the same Process level to catch and handle that error.
Cancel		This type of End Event is used within a Transaction Sub-Process. It will indicate that the Transaction should be cancelled and will trigger a Cancel Intermediate Event attached to the Sub-Process boundary. In addition, it will indicate that a Transaction Protocol Cancel message should be sent to any Entities involved in the Transaction.
Compensation		This type of End Event indicates that a Compensation is necessary. To be compensated, an activity must have a Compensation Intermediate Event attached to its boundary.
Link		An incoming token to this event is directly transmitted to the corresponding Start or Intermediate Link Event type.
Terminate		It indicates that all remaining activities in the Process have to terminate instantaneously. The Process terminates without compensation mechanism nor exceptions handling.

Type	Symbol	Description
Multiple		This event allows the multiple consequences of ending the Process. The trigger type is specified on its attribute.

Intermediate Event

The Intermediate Event is an Event used:

- To catch events when it is associated with the activity boundary. It is generally used to handle an Error, initiate the Compensation activities or to cancel a Transaction.
- To broadcast the Event information when it is placed directly on the Sequence Flow. Any incoming tokens trigger the Intermediate Event.

An Intermediate Event object is not located at the starting or ending position of a Sequence Flow. These locations are only reserved for the Start and End Event.

The Sequence Flow uses an Intermediate Event in the following situations:

- Handle the expected or sent messages within the Process.
- Handle timer event within the Process.
- Handle the exceptions or disruptions of the normal Sequence Flow.
- Handle the Compensation activities.

The graphical shape of the Intermediate Event is a doubled outline as illustrated in Figure 3.18.

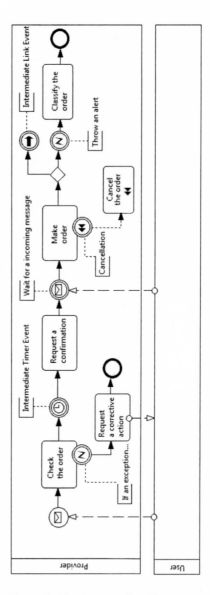

Figure 3.18 – Intermediate Event type

The BPMN specification describes nine Intermediate Event types as described in Table 3.6.

Table 3.6 – The Intermediate Event types

Type	Symbol	Description
None		It indicates one or more changes of states in the Process. It is also used also to check the Process execution.
Message		The current Sequence Flow execution is interrupted while it receives an incoming message from another Participant.
Timer		The Process is interrupted for a specified amount of time.
Error		This event handles (catches) or throws an Error. If it is placed within the Normal Sequence Flow, the Error Intermediate Event throws an error. If it is associated with an activity's boundary, it catches the Error.
Cancel		This type of Intermediate Event is used for a Transaction Sub-Process. This type of Event must be attached to the boundary of a Sub-Process. It shall be triggered if a Cancel End Event is reached within the Transaction Sub-Process. It shall also be triggered if a Transaction Protocol "Cancel" message has been received while the Transaction is being performed.
Compensation		This Intermediate Event is used to initiate and perform the Compensation activities. When used in Normal flow, this Intermediate Event indicates that Compensation is necessary.
Rule		This is only used for the exception handling. This type of event is triggered when a Rule becomes true.

Type	Symbol	Description
Link		A Link is a mechanism for connecting an End Event of one Process to an Intermediate Event in another Process. Paired Intermediate Events can also be used as "Go To" objects within a Sequence Flow.
Multiple		There are multiple ways of triggering the Intermediate Event, but only one of them will be required.

3.7.2 Activities

Activity

An activity within the BPMN specification is a generic term to describe the work executed in an organization. An activity is atomic or compound and they are both graphically represented with a rounded rectangle shape. The label located in the center of the rectangle describes the activity role as illustrated in Figure 3.19.

Figure 3.19 – The simple activity shape

The BPMN notation defines three types of activity:

- Process
- Task
- Sub-Process

A graphical marker distinguishes each activity type as illustrated in Figure 3.20. However, the Process type has no particular visual representation. The Business Process Diagram represents the Process or a set of Processes within their Pools.

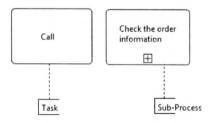

Figure 3.20 – The Task and the Sub-Process representation

The Table 3.7 describes the standard activity attributes. Some of these attributes are used during the Business Process implementation stage. The modeling tool set itself the value of the `ActivityType` attribute according to the modeler choice.

Table 3.7 – The standard attributes of an activity

Attribute	Description
ActivityType	An activity must be a Task or a Sub-Process.
Status	The status depicts the activity execution and may have the following values: None, Ready, Active, Cancelled, Aborting, Aborted, Completing, and Completed.
Properties (0-n)	These attributes allow the addition of specific modeler properties and extend the existing set. They remain internal to the activity.
InputSets (0-n)	Defines the data requirements for the activity input.
Inputs (1-n)	One or more Inputs must be defined for each InputSet. An Input is an artifact, usually under the object document connected to the activity.
OutputSets (0-n)	Defines the data requirements for the activity output.
Outputs (1-n)	One or more Outputs have to be defined for each OutputSet. An Output is an artifact corresponding to a document object attached to the activity.
IORules (0-n)	Zero or more expressions used to define the relation between the InputSets and the OutputSets. The instantiated activity with InputSets produces the determinated OutputSets.
StartQuantity	Specify the incoming token number required before starting the activity. By default, only one is necessary.
LoopType	This attribute specifies the instance execution iteration. The BPMN specification defines three types of loop: None, Standard and MultiInstance.

Task

A task is an atomic activity with the same shape as the activity. The BPMN specification defines several behaviors with the marker placed on the task shape as illustrated in Figure 3.21:

- The Standard Loop
- The Multiple Instance Loop
- The Compensation mechanism

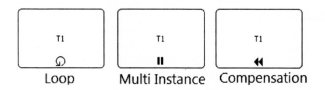

Figure 3.21 – The three task types

The BPMN notation allows the combination of the initial markers to obtain new task types like:

- The compensated looping task.
- The multiple compensated instances task.

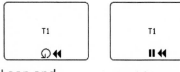

Figure 3.22 – Markers combination

The BPMN notation distinguishes several inherent behaviors within a task. However, that distinction does not visually appear on the BPD diagrams but only with the task's attribute `TaskType` that may have eight basic values as described in the Table 3.8.

Table 3.8 – Task behavior types

Attribute	Description
Service	The Service Task refers to an external service like a Web Service or dedicated software solution.
Receive	The Sequence Flow is temporarily interrupted and waits for an incoming message from another Participant. The Sequence Flow continues after receiving the message. Generally, the Process initiates its execution with the Receive Task type. It normally starts the Process and shares the same behavior as the Start Event.
Send	A Send Task transmits a message to another Participant. The task is finished when the message is sent.
User	An individual performs a planned User Task with the assistance of a Worklow engine.
Script	This Task contains an executable script available for the Business Process engine. The BPMN specification does not set the script language.
Manual	An individual performs the Task without the help of an automated tool.
Reference	If many activities share exactly the same behavior, the reference task reuses the same properties as the referenced task. The specific behavior is only created once and used from several locations.
None	The None Task is an undermined task that has no influence on the Process execution. It is used only to clarify the understanding of the Process.

The modelers are allowed to create their own task type with their markers as long as the basic shape remains the same.

Loop

A Loop type is a reiterated activity. The BPMN notation describes two types of Activity Loop:

- Standard Loop
- Multi-Instance Loop

The notation distinguishes the Standard Loop Activity from the task with a special marker in the bottom of its shape as illustrated in Figure 3.23.

Figure 3.23 – Loop activity sample

Table 3.9 describes the Loop activity dedicated attributes to specify the loop behavior.

Table 3.9 – Standard loop types attributes

Attribute	Description
LoopCondition	The evaluated Boolean expression for the loop execution.
LoopCounter	This attribute counts the number of loops at runtime. This attribute is incremented automatically by the Processes execution engine.
LoopMaximum (0-1)	Add a cap to the number of loops.
TestTime (before|after)	If the "before" value is set, the expression is evaluated before the activity begins like a "while" function in traditional programming language.

If the "after" value is set, the expression is evaluated after the activity ends like an "until" function in traditional programming language. |

The Multi-Instance loop type is equivalent to the programming language "for each" sentence. The loop expression is a numeric expression evaluated only once before the activity is performed. The Multi-Instance loop has an attribute called MI_Ordering that specifies the behavior of the instance creation:

- The *Serial* value means that it creates one-by-one the instances according to the Loop activity.
- The *Parell* value means that it creates concurrent activity execution.

Sub-Processes

A Sub-Process is a set of compound activities integrated within a Process. The BPMN notation distinguishes two graphical representations of Sub-Process as illustrated in the Figure 3.24:

- The *Collapsed* Sub-Process hides its internal detailed activities and uses the "+" marker.
- The *Expanded* Sub-Process displays its internal detailed activities and uses the "-" marker.

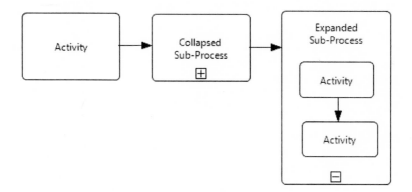

Figure 3.24 – Tasks and Sub-Processes

Generally, the modeling tools use the Sub-Process markers to change dynamically the appearance of the BPD diagrams.

The parent Process triggers the Start Event of the Sub-Process and starts its execution. At that time, the parent Process token is sent to the Sub-Process. When the Sub-Process execution ends, that token is sent back to the parent Process. If the Sub-Process contains concurrent Sequence Flows, it waits to retrieve all tokens before going back to the parent Process. Figure 3.25 illustrates the synchronization behavior with the expanded representation.

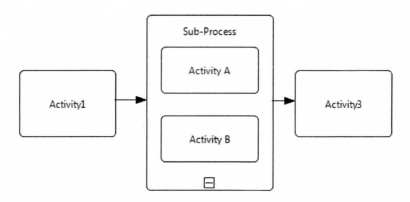

Figure 3.25 – Concurrent activity execution within a Sub-Process

It is not necessary to display explicitly the Start and End Event within Sub-Processes. However, it is commonly admitted that their representation helps to read the BDP diagram as illustrated in Figure 3.26.

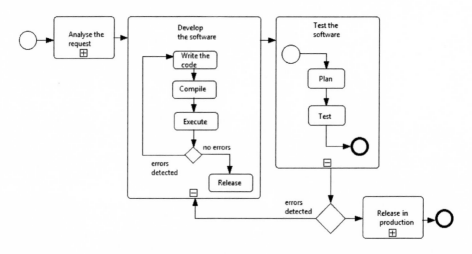

Figure 3.26 – Sub-Process in a BPD diagram

The parent Process execution works on global data. The integrated Sub-Processes have access and are able to manipulate these global data.

Sub-Process may have also additional markers to indicate a dedicated behavior as described in Table 3.10.

Table 3.10 – Collapsed Sub-Process markers

Type	Symbol	Description
Loop	Activity1 ↺ ⊞	The Sub-Process' activities are reiterated within a standard loop.
Multiple Instance	Activity1 ‖ ⊞	The Multiple Instance creates concurrent Sub-Processes according to the instance number specified.
Ad-Hoc	Activity1 ⊞ ∼	The Sub-Process' activities are executed without either a specific order or a Sequence Flow. The performers determine the activities' execution.
Compensation	Activity1 ◄◄ ⊞	The Compensation Sub-Process, linked with an Intermediate Compensation Event, contains the activities executed during the Compensation mechanism.

Flow and Connecting Objects included in a Sub-Process cannot have any Sequence Flows outside of the Sub-Process's boundary. However, the Sub-Process activities are able to communicate outside the boundaries with the Message Flows.

The behavior between the parent Process and its Sub-Process depends on the integration of the latter. The BPMN specification describes three ways to include the Sub-Process within a parent Process:

- The *Embedded Sub-Process* is an activity containing other activities or its own Sequence Flow directly integrated within the parent Process. It represents the most common way of Sub-Process integration in BPD diagrams. However, the Embedded Sub-Processes do not have all the features that the Processes have, such as Pools and Lanes. An expanded view of the Embedded Sub-Process would only contain Flow Objects, Connecting Objects, and Artifacts.
- The *Independent Sub-Process* is an activity calling another Process. The called Process is not dependant on the Sub-Process's Parent Process instantiation. The Sub-Process can be instantiated in parallel by other Sub-Processes. That behavior is equivalent to the sub-routine mechanism used in traditional programming language.
- The *Reference Sub-Process* allows the possibility of reusing and referencing an existing Sub-Process. In that case, it is only necessary to define the Sub-Process attributes to obtain the desired behavior.

Sometimes, it is necessary to ensure that all activities are executed within a single batch. That behavior is something like an "all or nothing" execution. The Business Process Management System that executes the Process provides the transactional protocol support. If something occurs during the Process execution, it ensures that all previously executed activities are rolled back and the Process returns to its initial state.

The BPMN specification defines the visual representation for transaction without describing the way to implement it. Transactional Activity or Sub-Processes have their outline shapes redoubled as illustrated in Figure 3.27.

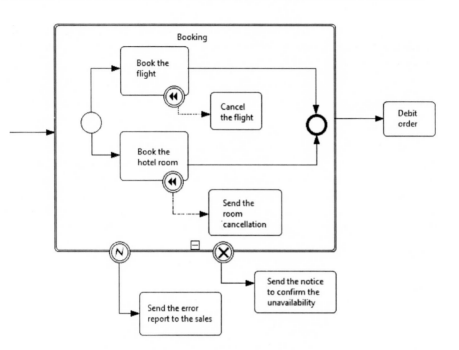

Figure 3.27 – Transaction expanded Sub-Process

There are three basic outcomes of a transaction:

- Successful completion displayed as a normal Sequence Flow that leaves the Sub-Process.
- Failed completion completed by a cancellation of the transaction. In such case, the transactional activities will be subjected to the cancellation actions, which could include rolling back the Process and compensation for specific activities. There are two mechanisms that can signal the cancellation of a transaction: a Cancel Event reached within the transaction Sub-Process or a cancel message received through the transaction protocol that is supporting the execution of the Sub-Process.
- Hazard refers to an abnormal situation not handled within the normal Sequence Flow or the cancellation mechanism. The Error Event supports that situation. When an Error occurs, it interrupts the activity and triggers the corresponding Intermediate Event.

When each transactional Sub-Process flow triggers an End Event, the token does not directly return to the parent Process as it does in the normal Sub-Process. The transactional protocol requires that all of its Processes reach the end of their transactions. If one of these is not able to end, all are redirected to the Intermediate Event for the rollback.

3.7.3 Gateways

A Process may contain several alternatives or concurrent Sequence Flows. The Gateway object controls the divergence and convergence of these Sequence Flows. The Gateway object may have many incoming and outgoing Sequence Flows also considered as Gates. For outgoing flows, the Gateway evaluates the alternative Gate based on a defined conditional evaluation. The general Gateway behavior is similar to the classical programming language "if....then...else". However, the Gateway type specifies the conditional features influencing its behavior.

The generic shape of the Gateway is a diamond as illustrated in Figure 3.28.

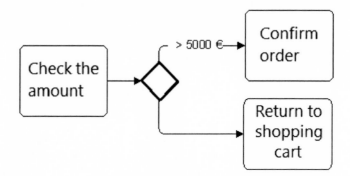

Figure 3.28 – The Gateway notation

The BPMN specification defines four Gateway types:

- Exclusive decision/merge (XOR)
- Inclusive decision/merge (OR)
- Complex decision/merge
- Parallel fork/join (AND)

The type of the Gateway is set with a particular marker placed in the center of the diamond. Figure 3.29 illustrates the Gateway types and their markers.

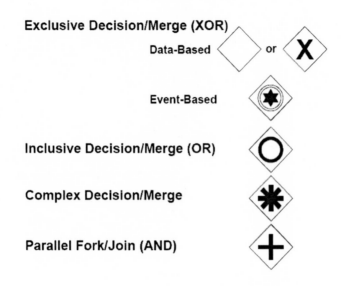

Figure 3.29 – The different types of Gateways

Exclusive Gateway

The Exclusive Gateway (XOR) has a similar behavior with the "either x or y" sentence in standard programming language. The Gateway chooses the Gate from an initial condition. The BPMN notation defines two types of exclusive decisions:

- A *Data-Based Gateway* has a Boolean expression evaluated from the information contained in the Sequence Flow. It is the most common Gateway type used within the BPD diagrams. The Data-Based marker is either left blank or contains a letter "X" as illustrated in Figure 3.30.

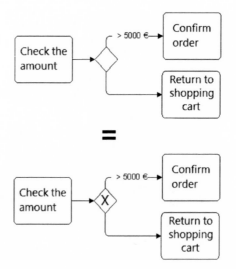

Figure 3.30 – Data-Based exclusive decision Gateway sample

- An *Event-Based Gateway* with the selection based with the event handled. Figure 3.31 illustrates the reception of messages that triggers the appropriate Sequence Flow.

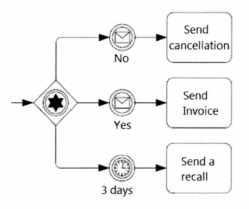

Figure 3.31 – Event-based exclusive decision Gateway sample

The Gateway evaluates the alternative Gates in a sequential order until the Boolean condition is true. The remaining unevaluated Gates are never tested once a Gate is chosen. A Gateway may have one *default* Gate as illustrated in Figure 3.32. The default Gate is represented with a Default Sequence Flow. Once specified, the default Gate is the last evaluated.

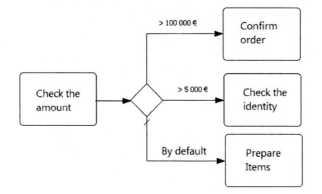

Figure 3.32 – Default Gate

The Exclusive Gateway is also used to merge alternative Sequence Flows. However, an activity can play that role too as illustrated in the Figure 3.33.

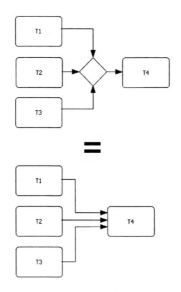

Figure 3.33 – The merge of several alternative Sequence Flows

Inclusive Gateway

An Inclusive Gateway (OR) evaluates all alternative Gates conditions and chooses the corresponding ones. At least one Gate has to be chosen.

The BPMN notation defines two graphical Inclusive Gateway representations. The first uses a Conditional Flow as an outgoing activity illustrated in Figure 3.34.

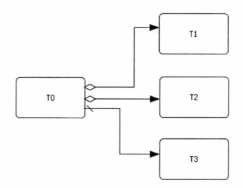

Figure 3.34 – Inclusive decision Gateway

The second representation of the Inclusive Gateway contains the letter "O" placed in the center of the diamond as illustrated in Figure 3.35.

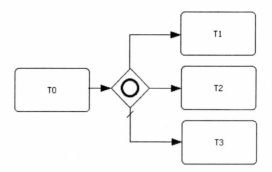

Figure 3.35 – Second representation of an Inclusive decision Gateway

An Inclusive Gateway can merge and synchronize several Sequence Flows as illustrated in Figure 3.36. In such case, the Inclusive Gateway waits for all incoming tokens before continuing the Process. This synchronization mechanism is only available for Sequence Flows previously initiated within an Inclusive Gateway.

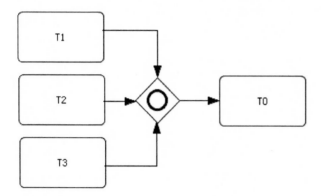

Figure 3.36 – Inclusive Gateway to merge Sequence Flows

Complex Gateway

The Complex Gateway supports situations that are not easily covered by all other Gateway types. Its expression will determine the outgoing Gate to let the Process continue. The Gate selection is made within a wide range of choices according to the expression evaluation. However, at least one Gate has to be chosen. A diamond containing an asterisk in its center represents the Complex Gateway as illustrated in Figure 3.37.

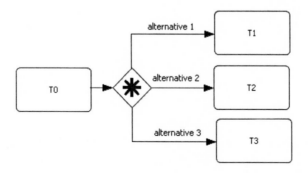

Figure 3.37 – Complex decision Gateway

The Complex Gateway may merge several Sequence Flows. The evaluation of the Gateway's expression defines the minimum condition on the incoming Flows to continue the Process. For example, an expression could define that "three tokens among five are enough to continue the Process". Figure 3.38 illustrates this type of Gateway within the synchronization of several Sequence Flows.

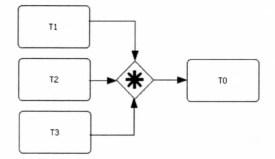

Figure 3.38 – Synchronization with the Complex Gateway

Parallel Gateway

The Parallel Gateway (AND) initiates or synchronizes several concurrent Sequence Flows. The Parallel Gateway contains a "+" marker as illustrated in Figure 3.39.

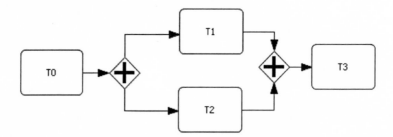

Figure 3.39 – The parallel fork (AND)

The BPMN notation describes an alternative representation of the parallel fork. In that case, the concurrent flows originate directly from the same activity as illustrated in the Figure 3.40.

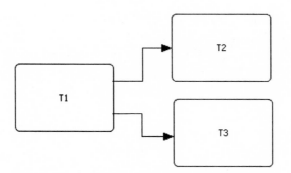

Figure 3.40 – Alternate parallel fork representation

However, it is recommended to use the Gateway shape in order to clarify the reading and understanding of the BPD diagram.

3.8 Connecting objects

The Connecting objects depict the links between the Flow Objects in BPD diagrams. The BPMN notation identifies three fundamental connecting objects types:

- The *Sequence Flow* links the Flow Objects within a same Pool.
- The *Message Flow* links Process Participants.
- The *Association* links the Flow Objects to the Artifacts.

The BPMN notation clearly differentiates these three connecting objects as illustrated in Figure 3.41.

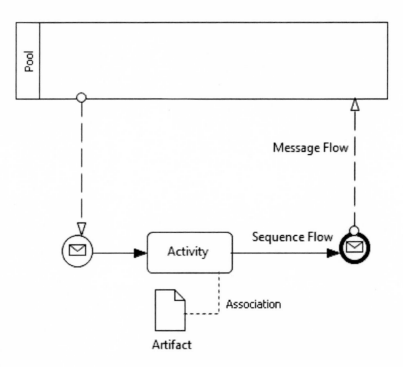

Figure 3.41 – Connecting objects

3.8.1 Sequence Flow

A Sequence Flow illustrates the sequential activity execution order in a BPD Diagram represented with a plain arrow between Flow Objects. Each Sequence Flow has a single input and output endpoint. It targets only Events, Activities, and Gateways objects.

The BPMN notation specifies several types of Sequence Flow representation:

- The *normal* flow with a continuous plain arrow describing the activity execution order.
- The *conditional* flow with a continuous plain arrow complete with a little diamond on its source endpoint. The Sequence Flow's attributes ConditionType and ConditionExpression define the condition to filter the tokens. The Sequence Flow is chosen when that condition is satisfied.
- The *default* flow with a continuous plain arrow having a 'slash' on its source endpoint illustrates the default Gate within a decision Gateway.

The BPMN notation clearly distinguishes these three Sequence Flow types as illustrated in Figure 3.42.

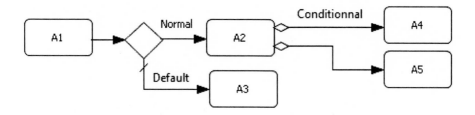

Figure 3.42 – The three graphical representation of a Sequence Flow

The BPMN specification differentiates between several kinds of Sequence Flow behaviors:

- The *Normal Flow* is an ordered sequence of activities beginning with a Start Event and terminating with an End Event. If there are no précised Start and End Event, the first and last activities play that role as illustrated in Figure 3.43.

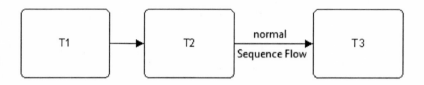

Figure 3.43 – Normal Sequence Flow

- The *Exception Flow* occurs outside the Normal Sequence Flow execution. It is based upon the trigger of an Intermediate Event, but not necessarily an Intermediate Error Event. That Intermediate Event is attached to the boundary of an activity as illustrated in Figure 3.44. The Exception Flow links that event to the specified activity E1.

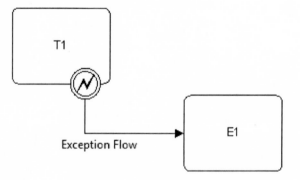

Figure 3.44 – Exception flow

- The *Link Flow* shrinks the Sequence Flow. Generally, the modeler uses that link to simplify the BPD understanding. Indeed, it reduces the number cross cutting wires in complex diagrams. The Link Flow uses the Link Event type as illustrated in the Figure 3.45.

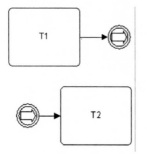

Figure 3.45 – Link flow

- The *Ad-Hoc Flow* executes the activities with an unspecified sequential order. The Process' users decide themselves upon the execution order. The Ad-Hoc flow does not have a dedicated relationship representation. Within a Sub-Process, the Ad-Hoc flow is represented with the "~" marker as illustrated in the Figure 3.46.

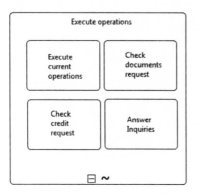

Figure 3.46 – Ad Hoc flow

The BPMN specification describes the associated Sequence Flow rules to the Flow Objects as defined in Table 3.11. The ↗ symbol indicates that the object listed in the row can connect to the object listed in the column.

Table 3.11 – Sequence Flow Connection Rules

From\To	◯	▢ Name	▭ Name	◇	◎	⬤
◯		↗	↗	↗	↗	↗
▢ Name		↗	↗	↗	↗	↗
▭ Name		↗	↗	↗	↗	↗
◇		↗	↗	↗	↗	↗
◎		↗	↗	↗	↗	↗
⬤						

3.8.2 Message Flow

The Message Flow depicts the information exchange between many Participants. An open arrowhead with a dashed single black line visually represents the Message Flow as illustrated in Figure 3.47.

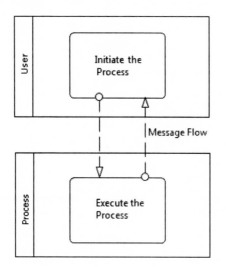

Figure 3.47 – The Message Flow

The Message Flow is used to:

- Connect the Pool boundaries.
- Connect the Flow Objects between Pools.
- Connect a Main (Internal) Pool to another Pool.
- Connect the boundary of Sub-Processes and Internal objects.

The Message Flow links together two or more Pools and their internal Flow objects according to the Participant type as illustrated in Figure 3.48.

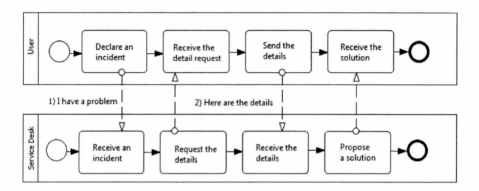

Figure 3.48 – The Message Flow usage sample

The BPMN notation specifies Message Flow Connection Rules as defined in Table 3.12. The ⤢ symbol indicates that the object listed in the row can connect to the object listed in the column.

Table 3.12 – Message Flow Connection Rules

From\To	◯	▤ (Pool)	[Name ▫]	[Name]	◎	◯
◯						
▤ (Pool)	⤢	⤢	⤢	⤢	⤢	
[Name ▫]	⤢	⤢	⤢	⤢	⤢	
[Name]	⤢	⤢	⤢	⤢	⤢	
◯						
◯	⤢	⤢	⤢	⤢	⤢	

3.8.3 Association

An Association links a Flow Object to an Artifact. A dashed line represents graphically that link in a BPD diagram as illustrated in Figure 3.49. The Association representation may have an arrow indicating the direction of the artifact usage. The Association does not influence the Sequence Flow execution.

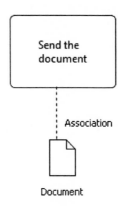

Figure 3.49 – The association representation

3.8.4 The Compensation Association

The Compensation Association is used when it is necessary to cancel a set of activities and reset the Process to its previous state. In such case, it is necessary to "undo" these finished activities. Generally, there are three ways this can be achieved:

- Restoring a copy of the initial values data and overwriting any changes.
- Doing nothing if nothing has been modified.
- Invoking some defined activities to undo the effects of the finished activities, also known as the "Compensation" mechanism.

The BPMN notation defines the Compensation mechanism as a set of graphical elements within the BDP diagrams. An Intermediate Compensation Event is placed in the activity boundary needing to be compensated. That Intermediary Event has a Compensation association set to execute the "undo" activities, rather than a normal outgoing Sequence Flow. The Compensation Flow is represented with a dashed arrow as illustrated in Figure 3.50.

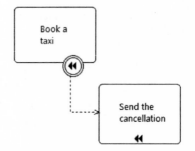

Figure 3.50 – The Compensation activity with "undo" activity

The activity associated with the Intermediate Compensation Event has no incoming or outgoing Sequence Flow. That Event can only be associated with one activity. However, it is also possible to use a single Sub-Process as illustrated in Figure 3.51.

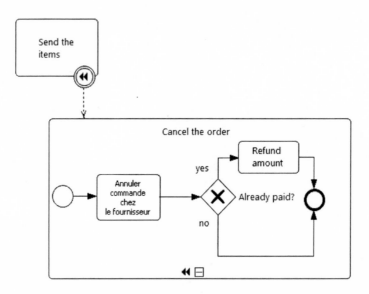

Figure 3.51 – Sub-Process as the compensation activity

Only the finished activities are compensated. There are two ways to trigger the Intermediate Compensation Event:

- The cancellation of an activity within a Transaction Sub Process. In such case, the Process flow will go backwards and any activities that require compensation will be compensated. When the compensation has been completed, the Process will continue its rollback.
- A downstream Intermediate or Compensation End Event "throws" a compensation identifier that is "caught" by the Intermediate Event attached to the boundary of the activity as illustrated in Figure 3.52.

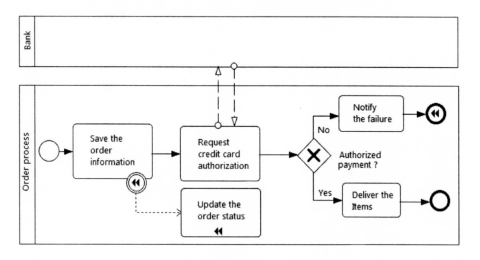

Figure 3.52 – Triggering a compensation activity

3.9 The Artifacts

An Artifact is contextual information added to the BPD diagram without any influences on the Process execution. The Association links the Artifacts with the Flow Objects. The BPMN specification defines three types of artifacts:

- A *Data Object* is an information structure generally used within the associated activity like a document, file, etc.
- A *Group* is a visual representation of a set of graphical objects used to show a special meaning of things.
- An *Annotation* is a simple piece of textual information used to attach a precise detail directly on the BPD diagram.

The modelers and modeling tools are allowed to add their own Artifact representations.

3.9.1 Data Object

The Data Object artifact is a bit of structured information placed within a BPD diagram. Unlike other notations, the BPMN specification does not define any Objects Flows for integrating the Data Objects. The Data Objects are only a representation of complementary information contributing to the general understanding of the BPD diagrams as illustrated in Figure 3.53.

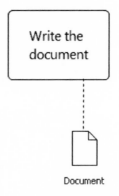

Document

Figure 3.53 – Data Objects usage in a BPD diagram

It may be possible to represent the transfer of a Data Object between two activities by associating them directly with that Data Object as illustrated in Figure 3.54.

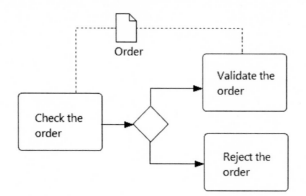

Figure 3.54 – Data Object used within a message flow

It is also possible to represent the Data Object direction usage within the Sequence Flow with arrows added to the Association link as illustrated in Figure 3.55.

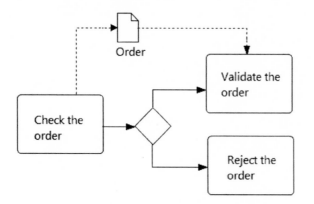

Figure 3.55 – Data Object direction

3.9.2 Group

The Group artifact is neither an activity nor a Flow Object. It cannot be connected or associated with any other graphical object. It is only used when it is necessary to represent a group of things to help the understanding of the BPD diagram as illustrated in Figure 3.56.

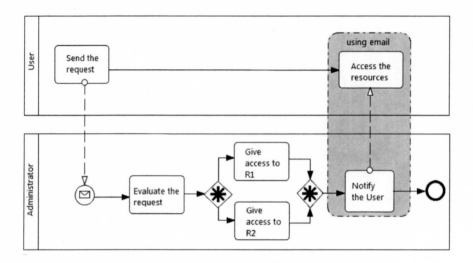

Figure 3.56 – Group artifact

3.9.3 Annotation

The Annotation artifact is a free text associated with any Flow Objects to help the understanding and reading of the BPD diagram as illustrated in Figure 3.57.

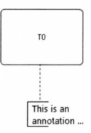

Figure 3.57 – The annotation

3.10 Business Process modeling with BPMN

The BPMN notation features are useful for the Business Analyst having to acquire and communicate the Business Process information. The BPMN specification also describes the translation of its defined graphical elements into execution language elements (BPEL4WS). It is easy to understand that the BPMN specification addresses two objectives: modeling and implementing the Business Processes. In order to achieve these objectives, the responsibilities are shared between two distinctive roles:

- The *Business Analyst* who drafts the BPD diagrams with a high level of business understanding.
- The *IT Developer* who adds sufficient technical details (BPEL, Web Services, etc.) to BPD information to ensure a correct execution of the automated Business Processes.

This book focuses on the Business Analyst role and describes only the graphical elements of the BPMN specification.

The BPMN specification defines the BPD core element set primarily for the Business Analysts within four categories:

- Flow Objects
- Connecting Objects
- Swimlines
- Artifacts

The Core Element Set contains three basic Flow Objects types:

- The None-type of Start, Intermediate and End Event in a business oriented event usage.
- The Task and Sub-Process Activity type without technical details. However, the Business Analyst may add some business details in the activities' attributes like the cost or the duration.
- The Exclusive Gateway indicates the alternative Sequence Flows in the Process.

The Business Analyst has three Connecting Objects:

- The Normal Sequence Flow displayed as a simple plain arrow between the Activities.
- The Message Flow used to represent the information exchanges between two or more Participants.

- The Association connecting the Artifacts to the Flow Objects.

The Flow Objects and Connecting Objects of a BPD diagram are placed within Swimlines:

- The Pool as the Participant.
- The Lane as the Participant's role.

The Business Analyst may add some Artifacts on the BPD diagrams:

- Data-Object
- Group
- Annotations

Figure 3.58 illustrates a high-level BPD diagram built from the Core Element Set.

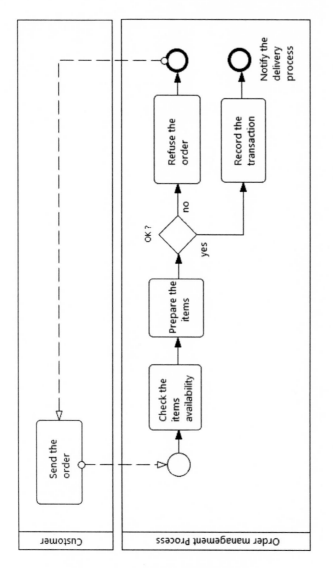

Figure 3.58 – High level BPD diagram

The IT Developer add enough details on the drafted analysis BPD diagram in order to implement the Process within an execution engine as illustrated in Figure 3.59

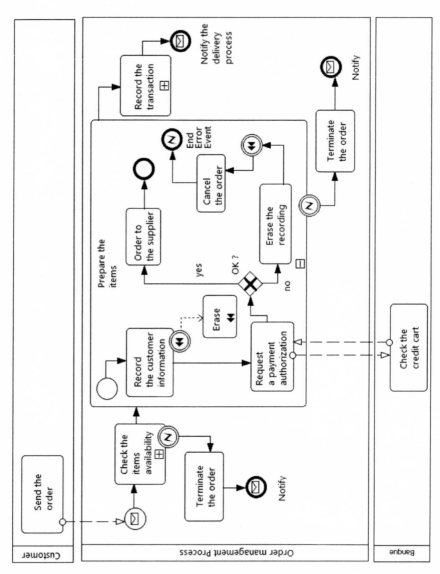

Figure 3.59 – Detailed BPD diagram

Chapter 4

Workflow Patterns

The Workflow Patterns address typical interaction behaviors such as generic flows. Wil van der Aalst, Athur ter Hofstede, Bartek Kiepuszewsli and Alister Barros have identified twenty-one fundamental Workflow constructions. Their complete work is available at the Internet address, http://www.workflowpatterns.com.

This chapter presents the twenty-one Patterns modeled with the BPMN notation. Table 4.1 describes the relationship between the BPMN flow categories and the Workflow Patterns.

Table 4.1 – The BPMN Sequence flows and Patterns matching

Sequence Flow	Related Workflow Pattern	Description
Normal Flow	Sequence	The flow is initiated from a Start Event and continues through activities via alternative and parallel paths until it ends at an End Event. The activities are performed sequentially.

Sequence Flow	Related Workflow Pattern	Description
Forking Flow	Parallel Split	It refers to the split of a Process into two or more concurrent Sequence Flows. The activities are performed concurrently, rather than sequentially.
Joining Flow	Synchronization	It combines several concurrent Sequence Flows in one path. A Parallel Gateway is used to synchronize two or more incoming Sequence Flows.
Splitting Flow	Exclusive choice, Multiple choice	It splits the path into two or more alternative paths (OR-Split). It is located within the Process where a question is asked, and the answer determines which of a set of paths is taken.
Merging Flow	Simple Merge, Discriminator, Multiple Merge, Synchronizing join, N out of M join	It combines two or more alternative paths into one path (OR-Join).
Looping	Arbitrary cycles, Milestone	It reiterates the chosen path.

4.1 The Sequence

The Sequence Pattern illustrates an ordered sequential activities execution as illustrated in Figure 4.1. The token is transmitted between activities along the Process. If the Sequence contains several concurrent and alternative Sequence Flows, it is necessary to join them to ensure that the latest activity receives a single token.

Figure 4.1 – The Sequence Pattern

4.2 The Parallel Split

The Parallel Split Pattern represents the concurrent activities execution. The Process splits its Sequence Flow into several concurrent Sequence Flows. This Pattern representation uses an AND gateway as illustrated in Figure 4.2. The path forking produces the same numbers of token as the number of concurrent paths.

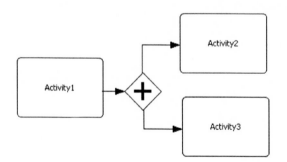

Figure 4.2 – The first representation of the Parallel Split Pattern

Figure 4.3 illustrates the second representation of the Parallel Split Pattern realized without a Gateway element.

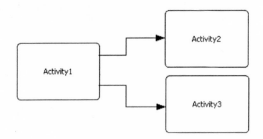

Figure 4.3 – The second representation of the Parallel Split Pattern

The BPMN notation allows the definition of concurrent activities within a Sub-Process object as illustrated in Figure 4.4

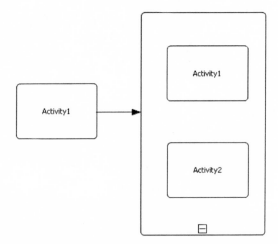

Figure 4.4 – The third representation of the Parallel Split Pattern

4.3 The Synchronization

The Synchronization Pattern combines concurrent Sequence Flows as illustrated in Figure 4.5. The Gateway object joins the previously created concurrent tokens. The Synchronization Pattern requests that all tokens be joined before continuing the Process execution.

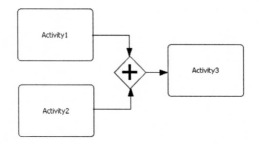

Figure 4.5 – The first Synchronization Pattern representation

The second graphical Synchronization Pattern representation does not use the Gateway as illustrated in Figure 4.6

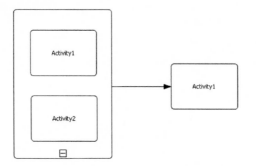

Figure 4.6 – The second Synchronization Pattern representation

Unlike the Parallel Split Pattern and its second representation, it is not possible to use a single activity to synchronize all incoming paths (cf. Simple Merge Pattern).

4.4 The Exclusive Choice

The Exclusive Choice Pattern is used when having to make a decision between several alternative Sequence Flows. This pattern is built with the Data Based exclusive decision gateway as illustrated in Figure 4.7. Once an alternative Sequence Flow is chosen, the remaining alternatives are not evaluated. At least one Gate has to be chosen.

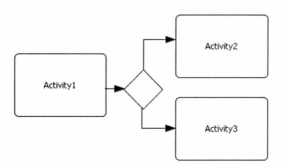

Figure 4.7 – The first representation of the Exclusive Choice Pattern

Figure 4.8 illustrates the second representation of that Pattern with the "X" marker placed in the center of the Gateway diamond shape.

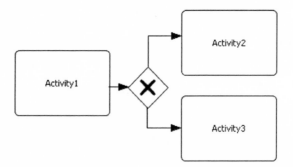

Figure 4.8 – The second representation of the Exclusive Choice Pattern

4.5 The Simple Merge

The Simple Merge Pattern merges many alternative Sequence Flows as illustrated in Figure 4.9. The Process continues its execution if the Gateway receives one token without consideration or synchronization of other tokens arriving from other Sequence Flows.

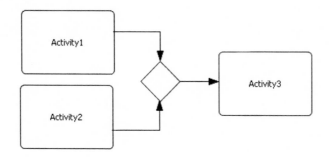

Figure 4.9 – The first representation of the Simple Merge Pattern

The second representation of the Simple Merge Pattern does not use the Gateway object as illustrated in Figure 4.10.

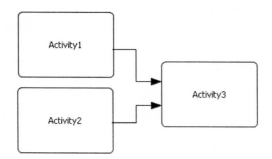

Figure 4.10 – The second representation of the Simple Merge Pattern

4.6 The Multiple Choice

The Multiple Choice Pattern selects the execution of one or more Sequence Flows. The BPMN notation offers two ways to represents the Multiple Choice Pattern. The first uses a collection of conditional Sequence Flows, marked with a mini diamond as illustrated in Figure 4.11. This Pattern needs at least one selected Sequence Flow. Each path evaluated with a true condition is selected.

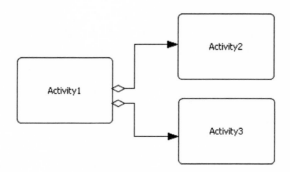

Figure 4.11 – The first representation of the Multiple Choice Pattern

The second way to represent the Multiple Choice Pattern behavior adds the Inclusive Gateway as illustrated in Figure 4.12.

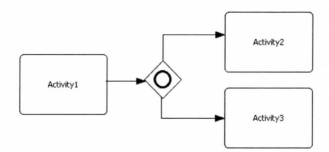

Figure 4.12 – The second representation of the Multiple Choice Pattern

4.7 The Multiple Merge

The Multiple Merge Pattern combines many Sequence Flows' tokens without controlling them as illustrated in Figure 4.13. An incoming token immediately starts the activity. If several Sequence Flows converge at an uncontrolled activity (Activity4), it may possible that the activity will be instantiated for each incoming Sequence Flow.

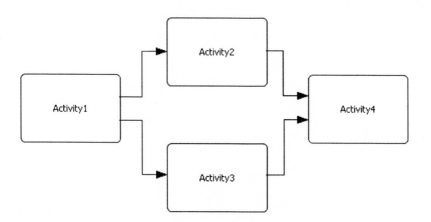

Figure 4.13 – The Multiple Merge Pattern

The Multiple Merge Pattern is different from the Synchronization and Simple Merge since they both produce only one instance of the target activity.

4.8 The Discriminator

The Discriminator Pattern is another way to merge many concurrent Sequence Flows as illustrated in Figure 4.14. The Process will continue if there is at least one decision taken among concurrent paths. The Process starts with many concurrent Sequence Flows. The first incoming Sequence Flow to the Exclusive Gateway is chosen and the Process will continue without consideration of the results from other concurrent Sequence Flows.

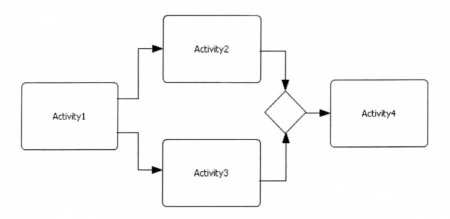

Figure 4.14 – The Discriminator Pattern

4.9 The N out M Join

The N out M Join Pattern depicts an alternative behavior of the Synchronization and Discriminator Patterns as illustrated in Figure 4.15. The Complex Gateway specifies the concurrent Sequence Flow selection conditions. The path that does not satisfy the specified condition is not taken into account for the continuing Process.

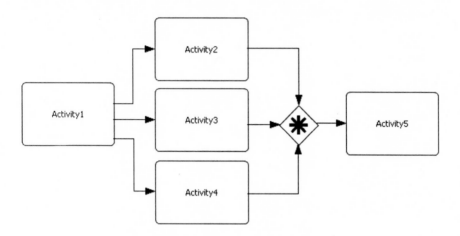

Figure 4.15 – The N out M Join Pattern

4.10 The Synchronizing Merge

The Synchronizing Merge Pattern is a variation of the Synchronization Pattern to synchronize all tokens from all concurrent Sequence Flows without having advance knowledge of the total number of tokens as illustrated in Figure 4.16. The Inclusive Gateway specifies that each path is independent and all combinations are possible, from zero to all. The second Gateway merges the first incoming path without consideration of the others.

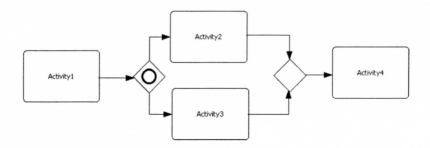

Figure 4.16 – The first representation of the Synchronizing Merge Pattern

Figure 4.17 illustrates the second representation of that Pattern.

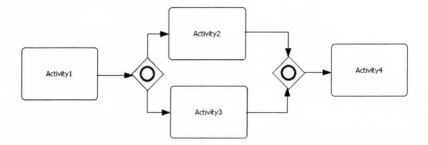

Figure 4.17 – The second representation of the Synchronizing Merge Pattern

4.11 The Arbitrary Cycles

The Arbitrary Cycles Pattern reiterates a part of a Sequence Flow as illustrated in Figure 4.18. This Pattern is built with a combination of Exclusive Gateways.

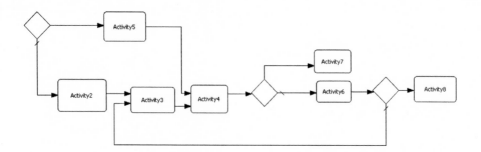

Figure 4.18 – The Arbitrary Cycles Pattern

4.12 The Implicit Termination

The Implicit Termination Pattern terminates a sequence flow without stopping other concurrent Sequence Flows as illustrated in Figure 4.19.

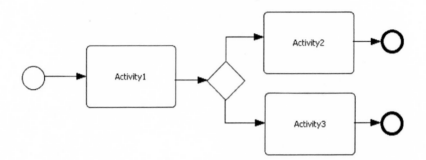

Figure 4.19 – The Implicit Termination Pattern

4.13 The Multiples Instances with a priori Design Time Knowledge

The Multiples Instances with a priori Design Time Knowledge Pattern describes how an activity can be simultaneously instantiated with a known number of iterations. This pattern uses the Multi-Instance Activity as illustrated in Figure 4.20. The modeler sets the number of times in the Multi-Instance activity properties.

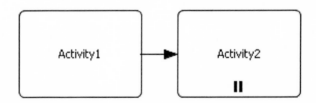

Figure 4.20 – The Multiples Instances with a priori Design Time Knowledge

4.14 The Multiples Instances with a priori Runtime Knowledge

The Multiples Instances with a priori Runtime Knowledge Pattern is similar to the Multiples Instances with A Priori Design Time Knowledge pattern, except that the number of copies is not known until the Process is being performed and cannot be set ahead of time. In addition, this Pattern can perform the activities concurrently or sequentially.

Figure 4.21 – The Multiples Instances with a priori Runtime knowledge

4.15 The Multiples Instances with no a priori Knowledge

The Multiples Instances with no a priori Knowledge Pattern differs from the previous Multiples Instances Patterns in that the number of copies of an activity cannot be determined before the creation of the copies. The exact number is determined during the instantiation of those copies. A standard looping or Multi-Instance Pattern will not be sufficient to create this behavior. A more complex form of looping is needed as illustrated in the Figure 4.22.

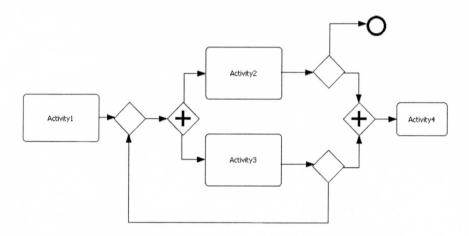

Figure 4.22 – The Multiples instances with no a priori Knowledge

4.16 The Multiple Instances requiring Synchronization

The Multiple Instances requiring Synchronization Pattern is similar to the Multiples Instances with A Priori Runtime Knowledge Pattern except that it requires that all the copies of the repeated simultaneous activity must be completed to let the Process continue. It is also built from the Loop activity as illustrated in Figure 4.23.

Figure 4.23 – The Multiple instances requiring Synchronization

4.17 The Deferred Choice

The Deferred Choice Pattern is an exclusive decision like the Exclusive Gateway. This Pattern is built on the event production during the execution of the activities as illustrated in Figure 4.24. The incoming event will execute one specific sequence flow. The Activity2 and Activity3 are Receive Task types.

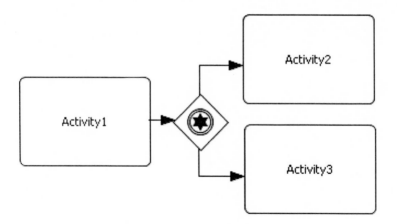

Figure 4.24 – The Deferred Choice Pattern

4.18 The Interleaved Routing

The Interleaved Routing Pattern sequentially executes many non-ordered activities as illustrated in Figure 4.25. This way of working is sometimes required when many activities share the same resources. The individuals in charge of these activities are responsible for giving the execution order.

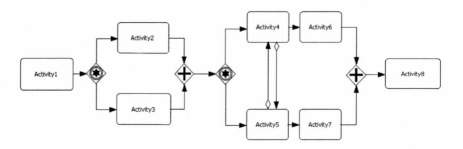

Figure 4.25 – The Interleaved Routing Pattern

4.19 The Milestone

The Milestone Pattern is used when it is necessary to know if an event is terminated or if specific conditions are met. A Milestone is inserted within the Sequence flow with an Event-Based Exclusive Gateway as illustrated in Figure 4.26. The Activity2 and Activity3 are Receive Task type. The Sequence Flow loops while the Activity2 triggers. When the Activity3 triggers, the Sequence Flow terminates.

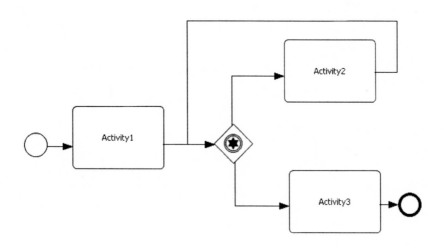

Figure 4.26 – The Milestone Pattern

4.20 The Cancel Activity

The Cancel Activity Pattern is used when it is necessary to terminate all concurrent activities if one of them is terminated. The controlled concurrent Sequence Flow contains an Intermediate Error Event as illustrated in Figure 4.27 with the Activity2. All other concurrent Sequence Flows contain at least one activity having an Intermediate Error Event in its boundary and acting as an event listener. When the Error signal is transmitted, all other concurrent Sequence Flows are immediately terminated.

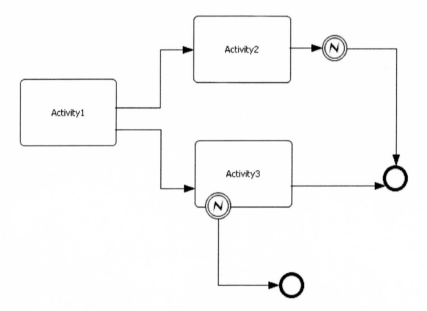

Figure 4.27 – The Cancel Activity Pattern

4.21 The Cancel Case

This Cancel Case Pattern is an alternative of the Cancel Activity Pattern. However, it cancels an entire Sub-Process as illustrated in Figure 4.28.

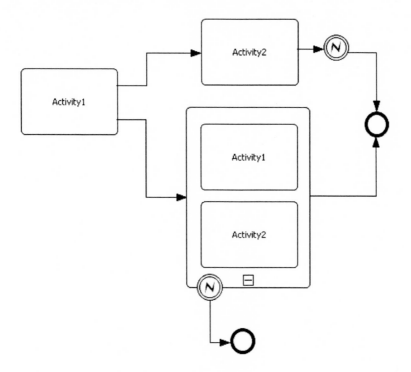

Figure 4.28 – The Cancel Case Pattern

Chapter 5

Samples

This Chapter presents four BPD diagrams illustrating the usage of the common BPMN visual elements. The fourth sample describes additional mechanisms supporting the Process implementation and execution within a BPMS engine.

5.1 Incident Management Process

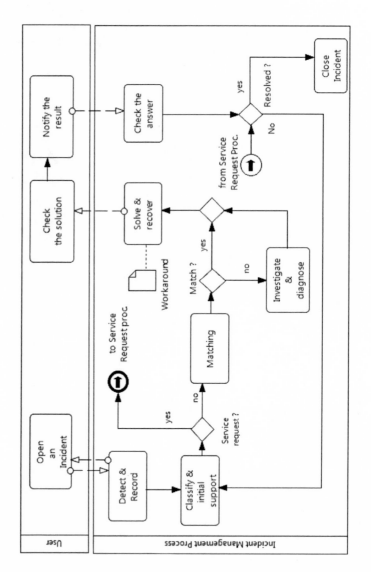

Figure 5.1 – Incident Management Process

5.2 Problem Management Process

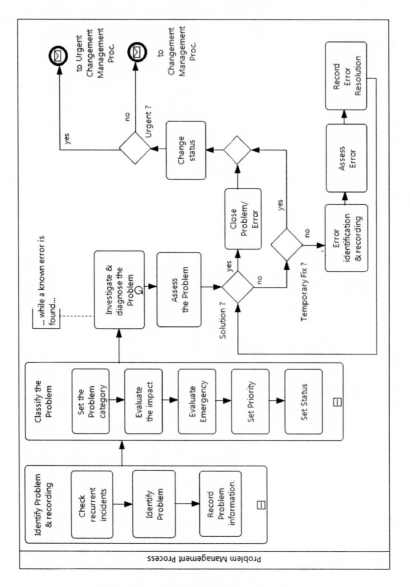

Figure 5.2 – Problem Management Process

5.3 Change Management Process

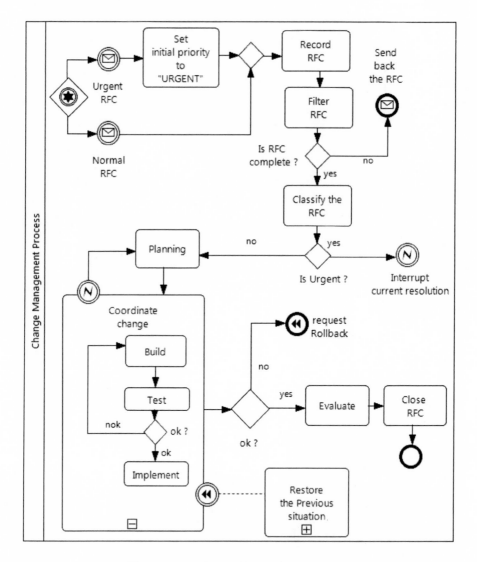

Figure 5.3 – Change Management Process

5.4 Receive Order Process

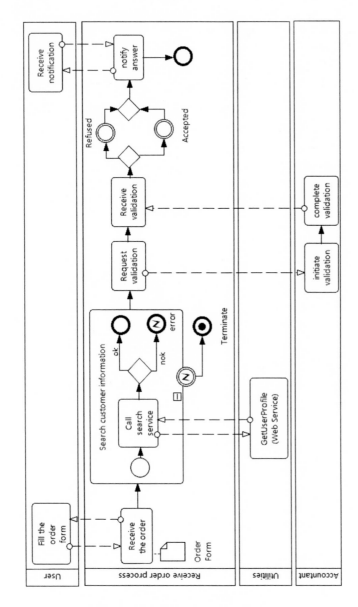

Figure 5.4 – Receive Order Process

The *Receive Order Process* illustrates common Process implementation and execution issues solved with the help of the BPMN elements.

That Process depicts an order request form filled by User and sent to the Purchasing Department. The labeled Receive Order Process Participant is an automated Process.

The Process requests the *Accountant* to check the validity of the order while the Web Service *GetUserProfile* retrieves the requester's information from a database.

The *Search customer information* Sub-Process checks the availability of the user profile Web Service. If that service is not responding, an error is thrown and the Process terminates immediately.

The None Intermediate Events log the outgoing status of the Accountant validation. That log is generally used by the Process Owner to monitor the Process execution. If these events affect one global data, the registered value may be used later on the Process execution to take a decision on an alternative Sequence Flow.

Chapter 6

Key differences between v1.0 and v1.1

An improved BPMN specification v1.1 has been released in January 2008. This chapter describes the key differences between the graphical elements of version 1.1 and version 1.0.

6.1 Graphical Element markers

The Table 6.1 describes the several changes applied to the graphical markers.

Table 6.1 – Graphical BPMN elements changes

Element	V1.0	V1.1
Multiple Event		
Event-Based Exclusive Gateway		
Multi-Instance Loop	Activity II	Activity III

6.2 Events Categories

The BPMN specification v1.1 clarifies the graphical distinction between the Event Transmitter and the Event Listener:

- The Event Transmitter "throws" or broadcasts the event information. This Event category is visually represented with black filled marker.
- The Event Listener "catches" the event information triggered by an Event Transmitter. This Event category is visually represented with unfilled marker.

Previously, the BPMN specification had no explicit distinction between the representation of Intermediate Event Transmitter and Listener. Now, the BPMN specification v1.1 clarifies that difference as illustrated in Figure 6.1.

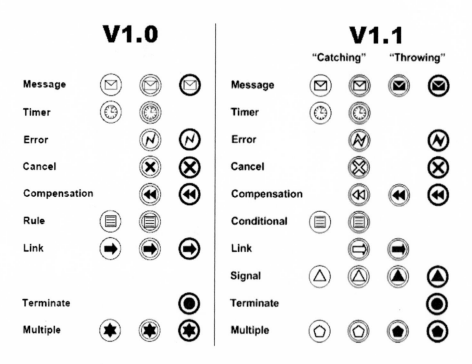

Figure 6.1 – Event types differences between V1.0 and V1.1

6.3 Signal Event type

The Signal Event is a new Event type introduced within the BPMN v1.1. A Signal is a mechanism used for the purpose of general communication within and across Process levels, Pools and between Business Process diagrams. A Signal is broadcast with no specific intended target. An Intermediate Signal Event triggers and executes the specified Sequential Flow if it catches that event. Even if the behavior is the same as the Error Event, it remains different since the Error Event is dedicated on special conditions while the Signal is used in a larger scope.

A Signal Event is available for all three main Event Types: Start, Intermediate and End Event types.

For example, Figure 6.2 illustrates the Cancel Activity Pattern with the replacement of the Intermediate Error Events by a Signal Events symbol.

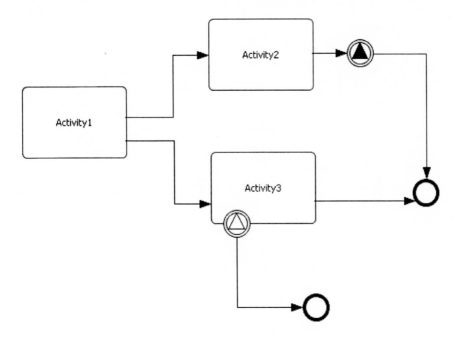

Figure 6.2 – Signal Event Sample

6.4 Link Event type

The BPMN specification v1.1 removes the definition of the Start and End Link Event types. It keeps the definition of the Intermediate Link Event type declined in both categories of the "catching" and "throwing" event. However, the Signal Start and Signal End Event type are able to replace the Link Start and End Event.

6.5 Rules Event type

The BPMN specification v1.1 renames the "Rules" Event Type to "Conditional" Event type. The graphical representation of that Event Type remains the same.

6.6 Event Details attribute

The BPMN specification v1.1 has changed the organization of the Event's attributes. Version 1.1 describes a common "Event Detail" property defined according to the Event Type.

- The Start and Intermediate Events type have the attribute *"Trigger (0-n) : EventDetail"*.
- The End Events type have the attribute *"Result (0-n) : EventDetail"*.

The EventDetail property defines the Event type: Message, Timer, Error, Cancel, Compensation, Conditional, Link, Signal, and Terminate.

As described in the Trigger and Result attribute, it may possible to have an EventDetail property zero or more. If there is no EventDetail, the Event type is a None Event. If there are many instances of EventDetail specified, then the Event type is a Multiple Event by default.

Figures

Figure 1.1 – Business Process Management life cycle.........................8
Figure 2.1 – Business Processes information levels...........................12
Figure 2.2 – Token flow between activities 13
Figure 3.1 – Sample BPD diagram..19
Figure 3.2 – Annotation in a BPD diagram 20
Figure 3.3 – Graphical objects used in a BPD diagram........................22
Figure 3.4 – Two Participants in the same BPD diagram 25
Figure 3.5 – Message flow representation between two Participants.............26
Figure 3.6 – Default BPD diagram Pool object...................................26
Figure 3.7 – The main BPD Pool 27
Figure 3.8 – Pool and Lanes within a BPD 28
Figure 3.9 – Private (internal) Process 29
Figure 3.10 – Private Process and their Participants 29
Figure 3.11 – Public (abstract) Process 30
Figure 3.12 – A set of Private and Public Processes 31
Figure 3.13 – Collaboration (global) Process....................................32
Figure 3.14 – BPMN Events sample 34
Figure 3.15 – Correlation set mechanism..35
Figure 3.16 – Start Event..36
Figure 3.17 – End Event sample 37
Figure 3.18 – Intermediate Event type 40
Figure 3.19 – The simple activity shape..43
Figure 3.20 – The Task and the Sub-Process representation.....................43
Figure 3.21 – The three task types 45
Figure 3.22 – Markers combination 45
Figure 3.23 – Loop activity sample..47
Figure 3.24 – Tasks and Sub-Processes 49
Figure 3.25 – Concurrent activity execution within a Sub-Process..................50
Figure 3.26 – Sub-Process in a BPD diagram 50
Figure 3.27 – Transaction expanded Sub-Process..................................53
Figure 3.28 – The Gateway notation...54
Figure 3.29 – The different types of Gateways 55
Figure 3.30 – Data-Based exclusive decision Gateway sample 56
Figure 3.31 – Event-based exclusive decision Gateway sample 56
Figure 3.32 – Default Gate..57
Figure 3.33 – The merge of several alternative Sequence Flows....................57
Figure 3.34 – Inclusive decision Gateway 58
Figure 3.35 – Second representation of an Inclusive decision Gateway 58

Figure 3.36 – Inclusive Gateway to merge Sequence Flows............................59
Figure 3.37 – Complex decision Gateway 59
Figure 3.38 – Synchronization with the Complex Gateway............................60
Figure 3.39 – The parallel fork (AND) 60
Figure 3.40 – Alternate parallel fork representation..61
Figure 3.41 – Connecting objects..62
Figure 3.42 – The three graphical representation of a Sequence Flow.............63
Figure 3.43 – Normal Sequence Flow 64
Figure 3.44 – Exception flow 64
Figure 3.45 – Link flow 65
Figure 3.46 – Ad Hoc flow..65
Figure 3.47 – The Message Flow 67
Figure 3.48 – The Message Flow usage sample..68
Figure 3.49 – The association representation 69
Figure 3.50 – The Compensation activity with "undo" activity 70
Figure 3.51 – Sub-Process as the compensation activity..................................70
Figure 3.52 – Triggering a compensation activity..71
Figure 3.53 – Data Objects usage in a BPD diagram 72
Figure 3.54 – Data Object used within a message flow 73
Figure 3.55 – Data Object direction 73
Figure 3.56 – Group artifact..74
Figure 3.57 – The annotation 74
Figure 3.58 – High level BPD diagram 77
Figure 3.59 – Detailed BPD diagram 78
Figure 4.1 – The Sequence Pattern..81
Figure 4.2 – The first representation of the Parallel Split Pattern 81
Figure 4.3 – The second representation of the Parallel Split Pattern.................82
Figure 4.4 – The third representation of the Parallel Split Pattern 82
Figure 4.5 – The first Synchronization Pattern representation 83
Figure 4.6 – The second Synchronization Pattern representation 83
Figure 4.7 – The first representation of the Exclusive Choice Pattern..............84
Figure 4.8 – The second representation of the Exclusive Choice Pattern 84
Figure 4.9 – The first representation of the Simple Merge Pattern 85
Figure 4.10 – The second representation of the Simple Merge Pattern............85
Figure 4.11 – The first representation of the Multiple Choice Pattern..............86
Figure 4.12 – The second representation of the Multiple Choice Pattern 86
Figure 4.13 – The Multiple Merge Pattern..87
Figure 4.14 – The Discriminator Pattern...88
Figure 4.15 – The N out M Join Pattern..89
Figure 4.16 – The first representation of the Synchronizing Merge Pattern 90
Figure 4.17 – The second representation of the Synchronizing Merge Pattern.90
Figure 4.18 – The Arbitrary Cycles Pattern 91
Figure 4.19 – The Implicit Termination Pattern..92
Figure 4.20 – The Multiples Instances with a priori Design Time Knowledge.92

Figure 4.21 – The Multiples Instances with a priori Runtime knowledge 93
Figure 4.22 – The Multiples instances with no a priori Knowledge 94
Figure 4.23 – The Multiple instances requiring Synchronization 95
Figure 4.24 – The Deferred Choice Pattern..95
Figure 4.25 – The Interleaved Routing Pattern 96
Figure 4.26 – The Milestone Pattern 97
Figure 4.27 – The Cancel Activity Pattern..98
Figure 4.28 – The Cancel Case Pattern 99
Figure 5.1 – Incident Management Process 102
Figure 5.2 – Problem Management Process..103
Figure 5.3 – Change Management Process 104
Figure 5.4 – Receive Order Process 105
Figure 6.1 – Event types differences between V1.0 and V1.1 108
Figure 6.2 – Signal Event Sample 109

Tables

Table 3.1 – BPD core element set 20
Table 3.2 – BPMN terminology 23
Table 3.3 – Event types 34
Table 3.4 – The Start Events description and symbol 36
Table 3.5 – The End Event types...38
Table 3.6 – The Intermediate Event types...41
Table 3.7 – The standard attributes of an activity...44
Table 3.8 – Task behavior types..46
Table 3.9 – Standard loop types attributes 47
Table 3.10 – Collapsed Sub-Process markers...51
Table 3.11 – Sequence Flow Connection Rules 66
Table 3.12 – Message Flow Connection Rules 68
Table 4.1 – The BPMN Sequence flows and Patterns matching.......................79
Table 6.1 – Graphical BPMN elements changes...107

Index

—A—

activities, 7, 11, 13, 14, 15, 17, 23, 24, 25, 26, 27, 30, 32, 33, 38, 39, 41, 46, 49, 51, 52, 53, 64, 65, 69, 70, 71, 73, 75, 79, 80, 81, 82, 93, 95, 96, 98

activity, 13, 14, 17, 20, 24, 25, 33, 35, 37, 38, 39, 41, 43, 44, 45, 47, 48, 50, 52, 53, 57, 58, 60, 63, 64, 69, 70, 71, 72, 74, 81, 83, 87, 92, 94, 95, 98

Annotation, 20, 21, 72, 74

Artifact, 20, 23, 69, 72

Artifacts, 21, 52, 62, 72, 75, 76

Association, 20, 23, 62, 69, 72, 73, 76

—B—

BPD, 19, 20, 21, 22, 23, 25, 26, 27, 28, 29, 30, 32, 33, 45, 49, 50, 52, 55, 61, 62, 63, 65, 69, 72, 74, 75, 76, 77, 78, 101, *See* Business Process Diagram

BPEL, 18, 75

BPEL4WS, 18, 28, 75

BPM, 5, 9, 10, 11, 14, 18

BPM life cycle, 9

BPMN, 5

Business Analyst, 8

Business Process diagram, 11, 14

Business Process Diagram, 19, 23, 43

Business Process Management, 7

Business Process Management life cycle, 8

Business Process model, 9

—C—

cartography, 9

Collaboration (global) Business Process, 28

Collaboration Process, 31

Compensation, 32, 38, 39, 41, 45, 51, 69, 70, 71, 110

Complex, 59, 60, 89

Complex Gateway, 54

Connecting objects, 62

Connecting Objects, 20, 51, 52, 75, 76

Correlation Set, 35

—D—

diagram, 9

—E—

End Event, 23, 33, 34, 35, 37, 38, 39, 41, 42, 50, 53, 64, 71, 75, 79, 109, 110

Event, 17, 23, 33, 34, 35, 36, 37, 38, 39, 40, 41, 42, 46, 49, 50, 51, 53, 56, 64, 65, 69, 70, 71, 75, 79, 97, 98, 107, 108, 109, 110

Exclusive, 55, 57, 75, 80, 84, 88, 91, 95, 97, 107

Exclusive Gateway, 54

—F—

Flow Objects, 20, 24, 33, 52, 62, 63, 66, 67, 72, 74, 75, 76

—G—

Gateway, 24, 54, 55, 56, 57, 58, 59, 60, 61, 63, 75, 80, 82, 83, 84, 85, 86, 88, 89, 90, 95, 97, 107

Group, 2, 17, 21, 72, 74, 76

—I—

Inclusive, 58, 59, 86, 90

Inclusive Gateway, 54

Intermediate Event, 23, 33, 34, 37, 38, 39, 40, 41, 42, 51, 53, 54, 64, 69, 70, 71, 75, 98, 106, 108, 109, 110

ISO9000, 10

—L—

Lane, 27, 76
Lanes, 20, 27, 28, 52
Loop, 45, 47, 48, 51, 95, 107

—M—

Message Flow, 20, 24, 62, 67, 68, 75

—O—

Object, 2, 14, 17, 21, 69, 72, 73, 74, 76
OMG, 2, 5, 17
organization, 5, 7, 8, 9, 10, 11, 14, 15, 18, 23, 24, 25, 27, 43, 110

—P—

Parallel Gateway, 54, 60, 80, 81, 82, 83
Participant, 24, 25, 26, 27, 36, 38, 41, 46, 68, 76, 106
Participants, 20, 24, 25, 26, 29, 30, 31, 62, 67, 75
Pool, 24, 25, 26, 27, 28, 62, 67, 76
Pools, 20, 25, 43, 52, 67, 68, 109
Private (internal) Business Process, 28
Private Process, 29, 32
Public (abstract) Business Process, 28
Public Process, 30

—S—

Sequence Flow, 14, 20, 23, 24, 27, 32, 33, 34, 35, 37, 39, 41, 42, 46, 51, 52, 53, 55, 56, 57, 62, 63, 64, 65, 66, 69, 70, 73, 75, 79, 81, 84, 86, 87, 88, 89, 91, 97, 98, 106
Sequence Flows, 13, 23, 49, 51, 54, 57, 58, 59, 60, 75, 80, 81, 83, 84, 85, 86, 87, 88, 90, 92, 98
Signal, 109, 110
Start Event, 23, 33, 34, 35, 36, 37, 38, 39, 46, 49, 50, 64, 75, 79, 109, 110
Sub-Process, 23, 24, 36, 38, 41, 43, 44, 49, 50, 51, 52, 53, 65, 70, 75, 82, 99, 106
Swimlines, 20, 23, 75, 76
synchronize, 14, 58, 80, 83, 90

—T—

Task, 24, 43, 44, 45, 46, 75, 95, 97
token, 13, 14, 33, 35, 37, 38, 44, 49, 53, 81, 85, 87
transaction, 52, 53
Transactional Activity, 52

—W—

Workflow, 5, 28, 79

Printed in the United States
132006LV00003B/155/P

9 781409 202998